T5-CBE-820

A Pinch of Thyme

Recipes from the
New Hanover Regional
Medical Center Auxiliary

This cookbook is a collection of favorite recipes,
which are not neccesarily original recipes.

A Pinch of Thyme
Recipes from the New Hanover Regional
Medical Center Auxiliary, Inc.

Published by
New Hanover Regional Medical Center Auxiliary, Inc.,
a not-for-profit organization whose mission is to develop,
encourage, and accept funds for programs and services
of New Hanover Regional Medical Center

Copyright © 1998 by
New Hanover Regional Medical Center Auxiliary, Inc.
2131 South 17th Street
Wilmington, North Carolina 28402

Library of Congress Number: 98-067393
ISBN: 0-9665428-0-0

Edited, designed and manufactured by
Favorite Recipes® Press
an imprint of

FRP.

P.O. Box 305142
Nashville, Tennessee 37230
1-800-358-0560

Cover Illustration and Book Design: Janet Brooks
Art Director: Steve Newman
Managing Editor: Mary Cummings
Project Manager: Jane Hinshaw

Manufactured in the United States of America
First Printing: 1998   7,500 copies

Welcome to historic Wilmington and the Cape Fear coast—an area rich in the heritage of the Old South, yet a vibrant growing part of the New South. You need much more than a "pinch of time" to sample the various attractions here: an exciting and alive downtown area, with the Cape Fear River, the battleship *North Carolina*, and the numerous historic houses; the Azalea Festival each spring and Riverfest each fall; the beach and boating activities at Wrightsville Beach and Carolina Beach; and the many and varied fine arts offerings around the area.

Yet with all this activity, we Southerners, whether newly arrived or third generation, take pride in our cooking and dining. This collection is our invitation to you to join us in our celebration.

Many of the recipes you find here are previously unpublished and well-kept secrets. Some have been handed down from generation to generation, some have been passed from friend to friend, and some have been taken from cherished family cookbooks. But all are enjoyed and recommended by the contributors.

A Pinch of Thyme is offered for your culinary pleasure by the members of the New Hanover Regional Medical Center Auxiliary, a volunteer organization whose mission is to develop and encourage funding for programs on the medical center campus. Some of the projects which have been supported by the Auxiliary in the past include "Main Street" in the Rehabilitation Center; the oncology program and the new Cancer Center now under construction; furnishings for the children's area; stained glass for the Chapel; and vans for the transportation of visitors.

The patients, physicians, and staff of the medical center are grateful to the Auxiliary for its continued support, helping to make New Hanover Regional Medical Center a place of excellence in health care for the patients and families of southeastern North Carolina.

Bon Appetit, y'all!

JOHN S. PACE, M.D.
President of the Medical Staff
New Hanover Regional Medical Center

Coming Home

When my wife and I returned to the Carolinas last year, we knew we had come home. Our senses were filled with the familiar—the sound of the ocean, the feel of the warm air, and the taste of southern food.

Food plays such a large role in how a place feels. A region's cuisine is as much a part of its character as its landscape and history. It comes from the people who live there, sharing recipes like favorite stories, passing them from friend to friend, generation to generation.

The recipes included in this cookbook are a reflection of the people who contributed them. Some are distinctly southern, others come to this area from far-away places. They come with stories to tell, of home and of family, of good times and strong traditions.

Although it's impossible to share all the stories behind these recipes, we hope they will become a part of your family's traditions, and the meals and memories they create will be something you recall whenever you think of home.

DR. WILLIAM ATKINSON

Contents

Introduction. 6

Appetizers ❧ Beverages 7
Soups ❧ Salads ❧ Breads. 21
Meat ❧ Chicken ❧ Seafood. 47
Vegetables ❧ Side Dishes. 81
Cakes ❧ Cookies 103
Desserts ❧ Pies ❧ Candy 131

Contributors List 154
Index 155
Order Information 159

Introduction

What is this wonderful herb called thyme? It's a common herb with small pointed leaves used to create culinary delights. In preparing a special dish, seasoning can make all the difference. At New Hanover Regional Medical Center, volunteers are the "special seasoning" that makes the difference in the way that many of the patients judge their hospital experience.

Volunteers use another type of "time" to bring delight to millions of people from all walks of life. Their time is used to bring a smile to the face of a child who misses his parents. An old person with failing eyesight may be comforted by a caring voice reading his favorite book or a letter from a family member or friend. Babies are comforted by soft hands holding them while they are gently rocked to sleep. Nurses are given the gift of extra time to tend a critical patient while a volunteer pushes another patient in a wheelchair. Volunteers, with smiles as bright as the flowers they carry, bring joy to the ailing patients when they walk through their doors.

These same volunteers must stretch their time to include husbands, wives, children, other family members, and the community. The next time you encounter a volunteer, take a moment to remember that as they use their "pinch of time" for others, they are the same people who use a "pinch of thyme" to make their family's lives more enjoyable.

All the recipes in this book were contributed by volunteers of New Hanover Medical Center and are another example of the countless hours and financial savings made to this institution by this group of hard-working, loyal, and dedicated people.

BETSY WATKINS
COOKBOOK CHAIRMAN

Appetizers
Beverages

A Husband Looks at the Pink Ladies

There goes Mother dressed in pink
While I head for the kitchen sink.
Children to feed, dishes to do,
Two hours more before I'm through.

Mother's in the Pink Lady shop
Leaning on the counter top
Chatting with the customers there
And being oh so debonair.

Other days she'll depart
And push around the coffee cart,
And return worn and thinner
To pull out a TV dinner.

Nonetheless I always cheer
For my little volunteer,
Because if I'm sick, I'll need, I think,
A doctor, a nurse, and a lady in pink.

Ham Rolls

4 (20-count) packages small
   rolls in foil pans

1 pound cooked ham, grated

1/3 pound Swiss cheese,
   shredded

1 small onion, grated

1 cup melted butter

1 tablespoon dry mustard

3 tablespoons poppy seeds

1 teaspoon Worcestershire
   sauce

Remove the rolls from the foil pans without
separating into individual rolls. Slice the entire
packages into halves horizontally. Place the bottom
halves back into the foil pans.

Combine the ham, cheese, onion, butter, dry
mustard, poppy seeds and Worcestershire sauce in
a bowl and mix well. Spread over the bottom halves
of the rolls and replace the tops.

Bake at 350 degrees until heated through; cut into
individual rolls to serve.

You may wrap the unheated rolls in plastic wrap and
freeze until ready to bake.

❧ YIELDS 80 ROLLS

Mexican Roll-Ups

16 ounces cream cheese,
   softened

1 (4-ounce) can chopped
   black olives

1 (4-ounce) can chopped
   green chiles

1 tablespoon chopped green
   onions

1/4 teaspoon chili powder

1/4 teaspoon salt

6 to 8 flour tortillas

Combine the cream cheese, olives, green chiles,
green onions, chili powder and salt in a bowl and
mix well. Spread on the tortillas.

Roll the tortillas to enclose the filling. Wrap in plastic
wrap and chill for 8 hours or longer.

Cut crosswise into slices. Serve with picante sauce.

❧ YIELDS 8 TO 10 SERVINGS

Mozzarella Cheese Puffs

1 cup sifted flour

1/4 teaspoon paprika

1/4 teaspoon salt

1/2 cup butter, softened

6 ounces mozzarella cheese, finely chopped

Sift the flour, paprika and salt together. Cream the butter in a mixer bowl until smooth. Add the cheese and mix well. Add the flour mixture and mix well.

Shape into small balls and place on a lightly greased baking sheet. Bake at 350 degrees for 15 to 20 minutes or until puffed and golden brown.

You may freeze unbaked cheese puffs and bake frozen, adjusting the baking time as needed.

❧ YIELDS 24 PUFFS

Pizza Rounds

1 pound ground beef

1 pound hot sausage

1 pound Velveeta cheese, cubed

2 tablespoons chopped parsley

1 teaspoon basil

1 teaspoon oregano

1/4 teaspoon garlic powder

2 loaves party rye bread

Brown the ground beef and sausage in a skillet, stirring until crumbly; drain. Add the cheese and cook over low heat until the cheese melts.

Remove from the heat. Add the parsley, basil, oregano and garlic powder and mix well.

Spread on the bread slices and place on a baking sheet. Broil just until bubbly.

You may freeze pizza rounds, store in a freezer bag and broil when needed.

❧ YIELDS 70 ROUNDS

Pickled Shrimp

2½ pounds shrimp

2½ cups chopped celery tops

½ cup seafood seasoning

3½ teaspoons salt

1¼ cups vegetable oil

¾ cup vinegar

2 cups sliced onions

8 bay leaves

2 tablespoons capers

2½ teaspoons celery seeds

1½ teaspoons salt

Combine the shrimp with water to cover in a large saucepan.

Add the celery tops, seafood seasoning and 3½ teaspoons salt.

Cook just until the shrimp are pink and firm; drain.

Combine the oil, vinegar, onions, bay leaves, capers, celery seeds and 1½ teaspoons salt in a 1-gallon glass container. Add the shrimp.

Marinate in the refrigerator for 24 hours or longer; stir occasionally.

Discard the bay leaves before serving.

❧ YIELDS 10 SERVINGS

Capers

Capers are the flower buds of a bush native to the Mediterranean and parts of Asia. The buds are sun-dried and pickled in a vinegar brine. Their pungent flavor is good in sauces, and they are used to garnish meat and vegetable dishes as well.

Hot Artichoke Dip

1 (14-ounce) can artichoke
hearts, drained, chopped

1 cup mayonnaise

1 cup freshly grated Parmesan
cheese

3 ounces bleu cheese,
crumbled

hot pepper sauce to taste

paprika to taste

Combine the artichoke hearts, mayonnaise,
Parmesan cheese, bleu cheese and pepper sauce
in a bowl and mix well.

Spoon into a 9-inch baking dish; sprinkle with
paprika. Bake at 350 degrees for 20 to 30 minutes or
until bubbly.

Serve hot with bland crackers or toast points or
spread on party rye bread.

❧ YIELDS 8 SERVINGS

Hot Cheese and Crab Dip

10 ounces sharp Cheddar
cheese, chopped

8 ounces sharp process
cheese, chopped

¼ cup butter

½ cup sauterne

2 (7-ounce) cans crab meat,
flaked

Combine the cheeses, butter and wine in a double
boiler. Heat over boiling water until the cheeses and
butter melt, stirring to mix well.

Stir in the crab meat. Cook until heated through.

Spoon into a chafing dish and serve with toast points.

❧ YIELDS 12 SERVINGS

Black-Eyed Peas con Queso

1 large onion, finely chopped

2 cloves of garlic, finely chopped

1/2 cup melted margarine or butter

16 ounces process cheese, cubed

1 (4-ounce) can chopped green chiles

2 (15-ounce) cans black-eyed peas, drained

Sauté the onion and garlic in the melted margarine in a large saucepan until tender.

Add the cheese to the saucepan. Cook over low heat until the cheese melts, stirring constantly.

Stir in the green chiles and peas. Cook until heated through, stirring frequently.

Serve with tortilla chips.

❧ YIELDS 12 SERVINGS

Guacamole Dip

4 or 5 medium ripe avocados

1/2 small onion, finely chopped

1 large tomato, chopped

2 or 3 cloves of garlic, crushed

juice of 1 small lemon

2 or 3 dashes of Worcestershire sauce

Tabasco sauce to taste

salt and pepper to taste

Combine the avocados, onion, tomato, garlic, lemon juice, Worcestershire sauce, Tabasco sauce, salt and pepper in a bowl.

Mash with a potato masher until mixed but not smooth.

Serve with tortilla chips and salsa.

❧ YIELDS 12 SERVINGS

South-of-the-Border Dip

1 avocado

juice of ½ lemon

1 pound tomatoes

1 medium red onion

1 bunch cilantro

2 to 3 small green hot
 peppers, seeded, finely
 chopped

salt to taste

Mash the avocado with the lemon juice in a bowl.

Chop the tomatoes, onion and cilantro on a glass surface and combine them in a medium glass bowl. Add the mashed avocado and mix well.

Add the hot peppers and mix well. Season with salt.

Chill, covered, in the refrigerator for 1 to 2 hours. Serve with white corn chips.

For hotter dip, include the seeds of the hot peppers.

❧ YIELDS 6 SERVINGS

Cilantro

Cilantro is the green leaves of the coriander
plant. The flavor lends itself to highly spiced foods
and it is widely used in Latin American,
Caribbean, and Asian cooking.

Layered Taco Dip

1 (14-ounce) can refried beans

1 large ripe avocado, mashed

2 cups sour cream

1 (1¼-ounce) envelope taco seasoning mix

½ cup shredded Cheddar cheese

½ cup shredded Monterey Jack cheese

2 tomatoes, finely chopped

1 bunch scallions, finely chopped

¼ cup sliced black olives

Spread the refried beans in a 10-inch plate or round tray. Spread the avocado over the beans.

Mix the sour cream and taco seasoning mix in a small bowl. Spread over the avocado. Sprinkle with the cheeses, tomatoes, scallions and olives.

Chill, covered, in the refrigerator. Serve with nacho chips.

❧ YIELDS 12 SERVINGS

Harvesting Herbs

Select undamaged leaves or sprigs just before
they flower. Freeze them immediately or
dry in bunches, then crush and store in airtight
containers for future use.

Rosedale Dip

2 cups (1 pint) mayonnaise

1 cup buttermilk

1 cup plain yogurt

2 tablespoons minced parsley

1 tablespoon lemon juice

½ teaspoon salt

¼ teaspoon onion salt

½ teaspoon garlic salt

Combine the mayonnaise, buttermilk, yogurt, parsley, lemon juice, salt, onion salt and garlic salt in a bowl and mix well.

Store, covered, in the refrigerator until needed. Serve with fresh vegetables.

This can also be used to top baked potatoes, asparagus, broccoli or salads.

~ YIELDS 1 QUART

Spinach Dip

1 (10-ounce) package frozen chopped spinach, thawed, drained

1 envelope vegetable soup mix

¼ cup chopped onion

1 cup sour cream

1 cup mayonnaise

Combine the spinach, soup mix, onion, sour cream and mayonnaise in a bowl and mix well.

Chill in the refrigerator for 8 hours or longer. Serve with crackers.

~ YIELDS 16 SERVINGS

Pineapple Cheese Ball

16 ounces cream cheese, softened

1 (8-ounce) can crushed pineapple, drained

¼ cup finely chopped green bell pepper

2 tablespoons finely chopped onion

1 tablespoon seasoned salt

2 cups chopped pecans

Combine the cream cheese, pineapple, green pepper, onion and seasoned salt in a bowl and mix well. Chill in the refrigerator.

Shape into 1 large or 2 small balls and roll in the chopped pecans. Chill for 4 hours or longer.

Garnish with chopped parsley or olives.

❧ YIELDS 12 SERVINGS

Strawberry Cheese Ring

16 ounces extra-sharp Cheddar cheese, shredded

16 ounces medium Cheddar cheese, shredded

1 small onion, chopped

1 cup mayonnaise

1 teaspoon red pepper

1 cup chopped nuts (optional)

1 (8-ounce) jar strawberry preserves

Combine the cheeses, onion, mayonnaise, red pepper and nuts in a bowl and mix well.

Press the mixture into an oiled 7-cup ring mold. Chill for 3 to 4 hours.

Invert onto a serving plate. Drizzle with some of the preserves.

Spoon the remaining preserves into a small bowl and place in the center of the ring. Garnish with additional chopped nuts and parsley.

❧ YIELDS 16 SERVINGS

Shrimp Mold

2 envelopes unflavored gelatin

1 (6-ounce) can vegetable
  juice cocktail

1 (8-ounce) can clamato juice

8 ounces cream cheese,
  softened

1 cup mayonnaise

2 (6-ounce) cans tiny shrimp,
  drained

1/3 cup chopped celery

1/3 cup chopped onion

1/3 cup chopped green
  bell pepper

Tabasco sauce to taste

Soften the gelatin in a mixture of the vegetable juice and clamato juice in a saucepan. Heat until the gelatin dissolves, stirring constantly to mix well; set aside.

Combine the cream cheese and mayonnaise in a bowl and mix until smooth. Add the shrimp, celery, onion and green pepper and mix well. Stir in the gelatin mixture and Tabasco sauce.

Spoon into an oiled 1-quart mold. Chill for 4 hours or until set.

Invert onto a serving plate and serve with crackers.

❧ YIELDS 16 SERVINGS

Chervil

Also known as French Parsley, this dainty annual with light green leaves and flat clusters of white flowers is often used in French cooking, soups, sauces and salads. It tolerates heavy frost and its tarragon/citrus/anise-flavored leaves can be picked any time to use fresh or dried and can be frozen for future use.

Shrimp Spread

8 ounces cream cheese

1/2 cup mayonnaise

1/4 cup (or more) catsup

1 tablespoon (or more)
    Worcestershire sauce

1 teaspoon lemon juice

1 small onion, minced

1 pound shrimp, cooked,
    cleaned, chopped

Combine the cream cheese, mayonnaise, catsup, Worcestershire sauce and lemon juice in a bowl and mix until smooth.

Add the onion and shrimp and mix well. Chill in the refrigerator.

Spoon into a serving bowl and serve with crackers.

❧ YIELDS 16 SERVINGS

Burnet

Often substituted for cucumbers in salads, burnet needs to be used fresh as it loses its flavor when dried. This perennial should be planted in poor, sandy, slightly alkaline soil and lightly watered and fertilized. It blooms in July with dense tufts of white to raspberry-colored flowers.

Vegetable Spread

1 small onion

2 large carrots, peeled

1 cucumber, peeled, seeded

1 green bell pepper, sliced, seeded

1 envelope unflavored gelatin

2 cups (1 pint) mayonnaise

¼ teaspoon salt

Combine the onion, carrots, cucumber and green pepper with water to cover in a blender. Process for 45 seconds; drain, reserving 2 tablespoons of the liquid.

Soften the gelatin in the reserved liquid in a bowl. Microwave the gelatin mixture for 20 seconds or until the gelatin dissolves; stir to mix well.

Blend a small amount of the mayonnaise into the gelatin mixture. Add the remaining mayonnaise, vegetables and salt and mix well.

Chill for 8 hours or longer. Serve with crackers or as sandwich spread.

❧ YIELDS 1 QUART

Lemon

The fruit of the subtropical lemon tree is well-known to us in many dishes or as a garnish, and can also be jellied. Its slightly bitter, citrus taste can complement a wide range of foods. The lemon tree's white blossom has a sweet, floral fragrance that permeates the orchard.

Champagne Punch

1½ cups sugar

2 cups fresh lemon juice

1 bottle Champagne, chilled

2 bottles sauterne, chilled

Combine the sugar and lemon juice in a jar, stirring to dissolve. Chill in the refrigerator.

Pour the chilled mixture into a punch bowl. Add the Champagne and wine at serving time, stirring gently to mix.

Garnish with sliced lemons or strawberries. You may add a liter of ginger ale if more servings are needed.

❦ YIELDS 25 SERVINGS

White Sangria

1 (1.5-liter) bottle riesling

1 (12-ounce) can frozen pulp-free lemonade concentrate, thawed

2½ cups lemon-lime soda

1 lemon, sliced

1 lime, sliced

1 orange, sliced

10 maraschino cherries

¼ cup maraschino cherry juice

Combine the wine and lemonade concentrate in a pitcher and stir to mix well.

Stir in the lemon-lime soda, fruit slices, cherries and cherry juice.

Chill for 2 to 3 hours. Serve over ice.

❦ YIELDS 10 SERVINGS

Soups
Salads
Breads

What Are Volunteers?

Volunteers are like Ford: They have better ideas.
Volunteers are like Coke: They are the real thing.
Volunteers are like Pan Am: They make the going great.
Volunteers are like Pepsi: They've got a lot to give.
Volunteers are like Dial soap:
They care more—don't you wish everybody did?
Volunteers are like VO5 hair spray:
Their goodness holds in all kinds of weather.
Volunteers are like Hallmark cards:
They care enough to give the very best.
Volunteers are like Amoco: You expect more and you get it.
But most of all, Volunteers are like Frosted Flakes:
They're G-R-R-R-E-A-T!

Cheddar Cheese and Asparagus Soup

8 ounces fresh asparagus, cut into 1/2-inch pieces

1 clove of garlic, crushed

3 tablespoons unsalted butter

3 tablespoons flour

4 cups milk

3 cups shredded sharp Cheddar cheese

2 teaspoons Dijon mustard

grated nutmeg to taste

1/2 teaspoon salt

1/8 teaspoon white pepper

Sauté the asparagus and garlic in the melted butter in a heavy medium saucepan over medium heat for 5 minutes, stirring frequently.

Stir in the flour gradually. Cook for 3 to 5 minutes, stirring constantly. Reduce the heat to medium-low.

Stir in 1 cup of the milk and the shredded cheese gradually. Cook for 5 minutes or until the cheese melts, stirring occasionally. Stir in the remaining 3 cups milk, mustard, nutmeg, salt and white pepper.

Cook just until the soup is heated through, stirring frequently. Discard the garlic before serving.

Garnish servings with additional shredded cheese.

You may substitute tender broccoli florets, cut green beans, green peas or pearl onions for the asparagus or add 1/4 to 1/2 cup sautéed red bell pepper for color.

❧ YIELDS 4 SERVINGS

Beef and Vegetable Soup

1 (16-ounce) can mixed vegetables, drained

1 (16-ounce) can whole tomatoes

1 (16-ounce) can yellow corn, drained

1 (16-ounce) can French-style green beans, drained

5 potatoes, peeled, chopped

1 onion, chopped

1 (16-ounce) can tomato sauce

2 cubes chicken bouillon

oregano, salt and pepper to taste

1 pound ground chuck

2 cups (or more) water

Combine the mixed vegetables, tomatoes, corn, green beans, potatoes and onion in a large saucepan.

Stir in the tomato sauce, chicken bouillon, oregano, salt and pepper. Bring to a boil.

Crumble the ground chuck into the soup, stirring to mix well. Add as much of the water as needed for the desired consistency. Reduce the heat and simmer for 1 to 2 hours.

❧ YIELDS 10 SERVINGS

Clam Chowder

1/3 pound bacon

2 quarts cold water

4 medium potatoes, chopped

1 medium onion, chopped

1 quart clams with juice, chopped

1/2 cup cornmeal

1 cup water

salt and pepper to taste

Fry the bacon in a saucepan until crisp. Remove and crumble the bacon, reserving the pan drippings.

Add 2 quarts cold water, potatoes and onion to the reserved drippings in the saucepan. Cook until the vegetables are tender. Stir in the undrained clams.

Mix the cornmeal with 1 cup water; add to the chowder. Season with salt and pepper. Bring to a boil and cook for 15 minutes.

Stir in the bacon at serving time.

❧ YIELDS 4 TO 6 SERVINGS

Squash Soup

3 cups chicken stock

3 pounds summer squash, sliced

3 large onions, sliced

6 tablespoons butter

1/2 cup heavy cream

1/8 teaspoon grated nutmeg

salt and pepper to taste

Bring the chicken stock to a boil in a 2-quart saucepan. Add the squash and onions. Cook until the vegetables are tender.

Process the mixture in batches in a blender until smooth.

Combine the puréed mixture with the butter, cream, nutmeg, salt and pepper in the saucepan. Cook just until heated through.

Serve hot or chilled.

❧ YIELDS 8 SERVINGS

Hearty Potato Soup

6 medium potatoes, peeled, sliced

2 carrots, chopped

6 ribs celery, chopped

2 quarts water

1 onion, chopped

6 tablespoons butter or margarine

6 tablespoons flour

1 teaspoon salt

1/2 teaspoon pepper

1 1/2 cups milk

Cook the potatoes, carrots and celery in the water in a large saucepan for 20 minutes or until tender. Drain, reserving the liquid and the vegetables in separate containers.

Sauté the onion in the butter in the same saucepan until tender. Stir in the flour, salt and pepper. Cook for several minutes.

Stir in the milk gradually. Cook until thickened, stirring constantly. Stir in the reserved vegetables gradually.

Add 1 cup or more of the reserved liquid to make the soup of the desired consistency. Cook until heated through.

❧ YIELDS 8 TO 10 SERVINGS

Fennel

A mild licorice flavor and looks similar to the dill plant characterize this perennial. Its leaves and large yellow flowers should be used fresh, not dried, in soups and salads. The seeds are used in beverages, baked goods and sausages, and the stalks can be burned to flavor grilled fish.

Turkey and Corn Chowder

4 medium onions, chopped

¼ cup butter or margarine

5 medium potatoes, chopped

2 ribs celery, chopped

2 cups water

1 chicken bouillon cube

1 tablespoon salt

½ teaspoon pepper

5 cups milk

1 cup half-and-half

2 (16-ounce) cans whole
    kernel corn, drained

1 (15-ounce) can cream-style
    corn

3 cups chopped cooked
    turkey or chicken

1½ teaspoons paprika

¼ teaspoon dried thyme

Sauté the onions in the butter in a large heavy saucepan until tender. Add the potatoes, celery, water, bouillon cube, salt and pepper.

Bring to a boil; reduce the heat. Simmer, covered, for 15 minutes or until the vegetables are tender.

Add the milk, half-and-half, whole kernel corn, cream-style corn, turkey, paprika and thyme. Cook until heated through.

Garnish servings with parsley.

❧ YIELDS 5 QUARTS

Apricot and Orange Salad

2 (16-ounce) cans apricot halves

2 (3-ounce) packages orange gelatin

salt to taste

1 (6-ounce) can frozen orange juice concentrate, thawed

2 tablespoons lemon juice

1 (8-ounce) can lemon-lime soda, chilled

Drain the apricots, reserving 1½ cups syrup. Process the apricots in a blender until smooth.

Bring the reserved apricot syrup to a boil in a saucepan. Add the gelatin and salt, stirring to dissolve completely. Stir in the puréed apricots, orange juice concentrate and lemon juice.

Pour the lemon-lime soda gradually down the side of the saucepan, mixing gently.

Spoon into a 9½-inch mold. Chill for 8 hours or until set.

Cut into wedges and serve on a lettuce leaf.

❧ YIELDS 12 SERVINGS

Orange

This perennial subtropical tree can reach up to forty feet in height and the strong, sweet fragrance of its white blossoms hints at its highly perfumed, citrus taste. It can accompany other fruits, salad greens or duck.

Grape Salad

2 (3-ounce) packages grape gelatin

2 cups boiling water

1 (16-ounce) can crushed pineapple, drained

1 (21-ounce) can blueberry pie filling

8 ounces cream cheese, softened

1/2 cup sour cream

1/2 cup sugar

1 teaspoon vanilla extract

1/2 cup chopped nuts

Dissolve the gelatin in the boiling water in a bowl; let stand until cool.

Stir the pineapple and pie filling into the gelatin mixture. Spoon into an 8x12-inch dish. Chill until set.

Combine the cream cheese, sour cream, sugar and vanilla in a bowl and mix with a hand mixer until smooth.

Spread over the congealed layer. Sprinkle with the nuts. Chill until serving time.

❧ YIELDS 15 SERVINGS

Easy Orange and Pineapple Salad

1 (3-ounce) package orange gelatin

12 ounces cottage cheese

9 ounces whipped topping

1 (11-ounce) can mandarin oranges, drained

1 (16-ounce) can crushed pineapple, drained

Sprinkle the gelatin over the cottage cheese in a 2-quart bowl and mix well.

Fold in the whipped topping. Add the oranges and pineapple and mix gently.

Chill for several hours. Serve on beds of lettuce. Add nuts along with the fruit if desired.

❧ YIELDS 8 TO 10 SERVINGS

Congealed Pineapple Salad

1 envelope unflavored gelatin

½ cup pineapple juice

3 cups drained crushed pineapple

juice of 1 lemon

1 cup sugar

6 ounces cream cheese, softened

1 cup whipped topping

Soften the gelatin in the pineapple juice. Combine the pineapple, lemon juice and sugar in a saucepan. Bring to a boil and remove from the heat. Stir in the gelatin until dissolved. Chill until partially set.

Blend the cream cheese and whipped topping in a mixer bowl until very smooth. Add to the pineapple mixture and mix well.

Spoon into a 9x9-inch dish. Chill for 8 hours or longer. Cut into squares and serve on lettuce leaves.

❧ YIELDS 12 SERVINGS

Pineapple Salad

1 tablespoon flour

1 tablespoon sugar

1 teaspoon salt

1 egg yolk

¾ cup milk

1 tablespoon vinegar

2 (16-ounce) cans pineapple chunks, drained, cut into halves

16 ounces miniature marshmallows

9 ounces whipped topping

½ cup chopped nuts

Mix the flour, sugar and salt in a small saucepan. Add the egg yolk and mix well. Stir in the milk. Cook until the mixture begins to thicken.

Stir in the vinegar. Cook until thickened, stirring constantly. Cool to room temperature.

Combine the pineapple, marshmallows, whipped topping and nuts in a bowl. Add the cooled dressing and mix well. Chill for 24 hours.

❧ YIELDS 8 SERVINGS

Dig-Deep Party Salad

5 ounces fresh spinach, torn

salt and pepper to taste

1 teaspoon sugar

6 hard-cooked eggs, finely
  chopped

8 ounces thinly sliced ham,
  chopped

1 small head iceberg lettuce,
  torn

1 (10-ounce) package frozen
  peas, thawed

1 red Bermuda onion, thinly
  sliced into rings

1 cup sour cream

2 cups mayonnaise

1 envelope ranch salad
  dressing mix

8 ounces Swiss cheese,
  shredded

½ to 1 pound bacon,
  crisp-fried, crumbled

Place the spinach in a large glass bowl and sprinkle with salt, pepper and half the sugar.

Layer the eggs, ham and lettuce over the spinach. Sprinkle with salt, pepper and the remaining sugar. Add the peas and onion rings.

Mix the sour cream, mayonnaise and salad dressing mix in a bowl. Spread evenly over the layers, sealing to the edge of the bowl. Sprinkle with the cheese.

Wrap with plastic wrap and chill for 8 hours or longer. Sprinkle with the bacon just before serving. Do not toss.

You may substitute tuna, crab, shrimp or lobster for the bacon.

❧ YIELDS 10 SERVINGS

Meat and Cheese Tortellini Salad

8 ounces meat tortellini

8 ounces cheese tortellini

1 (10-ounce) package frozen peas

1 red bell pepper, seeded, chopped

1 tablespoon olive oil or vegetable oil

1 large onion, chopped

3 cloves of garlic, sliced

1/2 teaspoon paprika

1 cup ricotta cheese

2 tablespoons tomato paste

1/4 cup grated Parmesan cheese

1 teaspoon salt

6 to 8 drops of hot pepper sauce

1/2 cup slivered basil leaves

Cook the tortellini using the package directions and adding the peas and bell pepper during the last 2 minutes of cooking time; drain.

Heat the olive oil in a skillet over medium-low heat. Add the onion and cook, covered, for 8 minutes.

Stir in the garlic and paprika. Cook for 4 minutes longer or until the onion is tender.

Combine the onion mixture with the ricotta cheese, tomato paste, Parmesan cheese, salt and pepper sauce in a blender. Process until smooth.

Combine the ricotta cheese mixture with the pasta in a bowl and add the basil; toss until combined. Chill, covered, in the refrigerator for up to 2 days, adding 1 to 2 tablespoons milk if needed to retain the consistency.

This can also be served warm.

➤ YIELDS 8 SERVINGS

Seashell Mold

1 envelope unflavored gelatin

¼ cup cold water

½ (10-ounce) can tomato
   soup

4 ounces cream cheese,
   softened

½ cup mayonnaise

1 (3-ounce) can tuna,
   drained, flaked

½ cup chopped celery

¼ cup chopped onion

¼ teaspoon lemon juice

⅛ to ¼ teaspoon sugar

Soften the gelatin in the cold water. Heat the tomato soup in a small saucepan. Add the gelatin to the hot soup and stir to dissolve completely.

Blend the cream cheese with the mayonnaise in a bowl. Add the tuna, celery, onion, lemon juice and sugar; mix well. Stir in the soup and gelatin mixture.

Spoon into a mold oiled with additional mayonnaise. Chill until firm. Invert onto a serving plate.

❧ YIELDS 4 SERVINGS

Easy Tomato Aspic

2 (16-ounce) cans stewed
   tomatoes

2 (3-ounce) packages sugar-
   free lemon gelatin

¼ cup wine vinegar

Bring the tomatoes to a boil in a saucepan, crushing with a spoon and removing any hard portions.

Add the gelatin to the hot tomatoes, stirring until dissolved. Add the wine vinegar. Spoon into a mold.

Chill in the refrigerator for 8 hours or longer. Invert onto a serving plate.

Garnish servings with mayonnaise.

❧ YIELDS 8 SERVINGS

Marinated Bean Salad

½ cup vegetable oil

¾ cup tarragon vinegar

¾ cup sugar

1½ teaspoons salt

½ teaspoon pepper

1 (16-ounce) can cut green
  beans

1 (16-ounce) can Shoe Peg
  corn

1 (16-ounce) can peas

1 green bell pepper, chopped

1 cup chopped celery

1 onion, sliced into rings

2 pimentos, chopped

Combine the oil, vinegar, sugar, salt and pepper in a bowl for the marinade; mix well and set aside.

Drain the green beans, corn and peas. Combine with the green pepper, celery, onion and pimentos in a large bowl. Add the marinade and mix well.

Marinate in the refrigerator for 1 to 2 days. Drain before serving.

To double the recipe, it is not necessary to double the marinade.

❧ YIELDS 8 TO 10 SERVINGS

Herbal Vinegars

Herbal vinegars are made by adding tarragon, rosemary, lavender, dill or other herbs of your choice to cider or wine vinegar and sealing in an airtight bottle. These vinegars are very good for salads or marinades.

Bibb Lettuce with Soy-Sesame Vinaigrette

2½ tablespoons tarragon
    vinegar

2½ tablespoons Japanese soy
    sauce

⅛ teaspoon dry mustard

⅛ teaspoon kosher salt

freshly ground pepper to taste

¼ cup olive oil

⅛ teaspoon (scant) sesame oil

¼ teaspoon chopped
    tarragon leaves

leaves of 6 heads Bibb lettuce

Whisk the vinegar, soy sauce, dry mustard, kosher salt and pepper in a small bowl until smooth.

Whisk in the olive oil, sesame oil and tarragon.

Toss with the lettuce in a salad bowl and serve immediately.

❧ YIELDS 6 SERVINGS

Corn Bread Salad

1 (7-ounce) package corn
    bread mix

1 medium tomato, chopped

1 green bell pepper, chopped

1 rib celery, chopped

1 green onion, chopped

½ jar bacon bits

mayonnaise

Prepare and bake the corn bread mix using the package directions. Crumble the corn bread into a bowl.

Add the tomato, green pepper, celery, green onion and bacon bits. Stir in enough mayonnaise to moisten.

❧ YIELDS 6 SERVINGS

Old South Cabbage Slaw

3/4 cup vegetable oil

1 cup apple cider vinegar

1 cup sugar

2 teaspoons dry mustard

2 teaspoons celery seeds

salt and pepper to taste

1 large cabbage, shredded

1 large onion, sliced into rings

2 medium green bell peppers,
   coarsely chopped

Combine the oil, vinegar and sugar in a saucepan. Bring to a boil over low heat. Boil for 5 minutes.

Add the dry mustard, celery seeds, salt and pepper. Cool slightly.

Combine the cabbage, onion and green peppers in a bowl. Add the dressing and mix well.

Marinate, covered, in the refrigerator for 24 hours.

❧ YIELDS 10 SERVINGS

Dry Mustard

Dry or powdered mustard is finely ground mustard seed. Its pungent flavor complements sauces, salads, and main dishes.

Asian Coleslaw

1/4 cup vegetable oil

3 tablespoons vinegar

2 tablespoons sugar

1 (3-ounce) package ramen
   noodles

1 (10-ounce) package angel
   hair coleslaw

1 or 2 carrots, thinly sliced

4 scallions with tops, chopped

1/3 cup sunflower seed kernels

1 teaspoon sesame seeds

1/3 cup toasted slivered
   almonds

Combine the oil, vinegar and sugar in a small
bowl and mix well. Stir in the seasoning packet
from the noodles.

Combine the coleslaw, carrots, scallions, sunflower
seed kernels, sesame seeds and almonds in a
salad bowl.

Add the dressing mixture and toss to mix well.

Crush the noodles and add just before serving.

Substitute very thinly sliced cabbage if the angel hair
coleslaw is not available.

❧ YIELDS 6 TO 8 SERVINGS

Borage

Both the leaves and bright blue star-shaped flowers of
borage have a cucumber-like flavor and are often used in
salads, but the flowers may also be floated in drinks
or candied for a dessert garnish. It can be grown from
seeds planted in early May. Use the leaves sparingly
as large amounts may be toxic and both should be
used fresh as they store poorly.

Greek Salad

2 heads Romaine lettuce,
coarsely chopped

1 bunch scallions, chopped

1 small Bermuda onion, sliced
into rings

4 radishes, sliced

12 imported black olives

12 cherry tomatoes, cut into
halves

6 to 8 tablespoons olive oil

juice of 2 lemons

1/4 teaspoon oregano

Jane's Krazy Mixed-Up Salt
to taste

Jane's Krazy Mixed-Up
Pepper to taste

1/2 cup crumbled feta cheese

Combine the lettuce, scallions, onion, radishes, black olives and tomatoes in a large salad bowl.

Mix the olive oil, lemon juice, oregano, salt and pepper in a small bowl. Add to the salad and toss to mix well.

Add the feta cheese and toss lightly.

⟜ YIELDS 6 SERVINGS

Oregano

The darling of Mediterranean recipes, this pungent perennial can be used fresh or dried. It blooms June through August with white, pink or purple flowers similar to marjoram, but is heavier-tasting, hotter and spicier.

Layered Salad

1 head lettuce

1 cup chopped celery

4 hard-cooked eggs, sliced

1 (10-ounce) package frozen
   peas

½ cup chopped green bell
   pepper

1 medium sweet onion,
   chopped

8 slices bacon, crisp-fried,
   crumbled

2 cups mayonnaise

2 tablespoons sugar

1 cup shredded sharp
   Cheddar cheese

Tear the lettuce into a serving bowl. Layer the celery, eggs, peas, green pepper, onion and bacon over the lettuce.

Combine the mayonnaise and sugar in a small bowl and mix well. Spread over the layers, sealing to the edge of the bowl.

Chill, covered, for 8 hours to 3 days. Sprinkle with the cheese just before serving.

❧ YIELDS 10 TO 12 SERVINGS

Sweet Onions

A number of sweet onions have been developed primarily in the western hemisphere. Among these are the Vidalia from Georgia, the Maui from Hawaii, the Walla Walla from Washington, the Oso Sweet from South America, and the Rio Sweet from the Rio Grande valley.

Broccoli Corn Bread

1 (10-ounce) package frozen
   chopped broccoli

2 tablespoons water

1 (7-ounce) package corn
   bread mix

6 ounces cottage cheese

1 large onion, chopped

4 eggs, beaten

1 cup shredded Cheddar
   cheese

1 teaspoon salt

½ cup melted margarine

Combine the broccoli with the water in a microwave-safe bowl. Microwave for 3 minutes; drain.

Combine the corn bread mix, cottage cheese, onion, eggs, Cheddar cheese and salt in a bowl; mix well.

Stir in the broccoli and melted margarine. Spoon into a greased 9x13-inch baking pan.

Bake at 350 degrees for 35 minutes or until golden brown.

❧ YIELDS 12 SERVINGS

Calendula

The ray petal is the edible portion of the yellow-orange calendula blossom and provides an attractive garnish. It is often used to color butter and cheese and is commonly known as the pot marigold. This hardy annual can be used as a substitute for saffron in rice or to flavor winter soups, custards or corn bread with a tangy, peppery taste. The petals may be used to rejuvenate the skin and relieve sunburn.

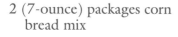

Corny Corn Bread

2 (7-ounce) packages corn
  bread mix

3 eggs

½ cup canola oil

8 ounces sour cream

1 (16-ounce) can cream-style
  corn

Combine the corn bread mix, eggs, oil, sour cream
and corn in a mixer bowl and mix until smooth.

Spoon into a 9x13-inch baking pan sprayed with
nonstick cooking spray. Bake at 350 degrees for
30 to 40 minutes or until golden brown.

🕊 YIELDS 12 SERVINGS

Cornmeal Muffins

1½ cups medium-grind white
  cornmeal

½ cup flour

2 teaspoons baking powder

2 teaspoons sugar

2 teaspoons salt

1 cup milk

2 eggs

2 tablespoons vegetable oil

Mix the cornmeal, flour, baking powder, sugar and
salt in a bowl.

Add the milk, eggs and oil and stir until smooth.
Spoon into nonstick muffin cups.

Bake at 400 degrees for 20 to 25 minutes or until
golden brown.

🕊 YIELDS 18 MUFFINS

Banana Nut Bread

½ cup shortening

1 cup sugar

2 eggs

1½ cups mashed bananas

2 cups flour

1 teaspoon baking soda

1 teaspoon salt

½ teaspoon vanilla extract

⅔ cup chopped nuts

Cream the shortening and sugar in a mixer bowl until light and fluffy. Beat in the eggs.

Add the bananas and mix well. Add the flour, baking soda, salt and vanilla and mix until smooth. Stir in the nuts.

Spoon into a greased and floured 5x7-inch loaf pan. Bake at 300 degrees for 1 hour or until a tester inserted in the center comes out nearly clean. Remove to a wire rack to cool.

You may bake this in 2 smaller loaf pans if preferred.

✒ YIELDS 1 LARGE LOAF OR 2 SMALL LOAVES

Violet

Like the Johnny-jump-up and pansy, the violet is a member of the viola family, but is a hardy perennial and has a sweeter, stronger scent. Its purple and purple-veined white flowers and heart-shaped leaves can be used as a garnish. The flowers can be made into violet water which can flavor tea, breads, fruit compotes and chilled soups.

Blueberry Bread

2 cups flour

1 cup sugar

1 teaspoon baking powder

1/4 teaspoon baking soda

1/4 teaspoon salt

2 tablespoons melted light
  margarine

1/4 cup hot water

1/2 cup orange juice

1 tablespoon grated orange
  peel (optional)

1/4 cup egg substitute

1 cup fresh blueberries

2 tablespoons honey

2 tablespoons orange juice

1/2 teaspoon grated orange
  peel

Mix the flour, sugar, baking powder, baking soda and salt in a medium bowl.

Combine the margarine, hot water, 1/2 cup orange juice, 1 tablespoon orange peel and egg substitute in a large bowl; stir to mix well. Fold in the dry ingredients. Fold in the blueberries.

Spoon into a 5x9-inch loaf pan sprayed with nonstick cooking spray and floured. Bake at 350 degrees for 50 to 60 minutes or until golden brown. Remove to a wire rack.

Combine the honey, 2 tablespoons orange juice and 1/2 teaspoon orange peel in a small saucepan. Bring to a boil and cook for 1 minute. Spread over the bread.

❧ YIELDS 12 SERVINGS

Cloves

Cloves are actually the sun-dried unopened flower buds
of the clove tree. Clove oil is used as a flavoring,
as an insecticide and as a numbing agent for toothaches.

Blueberry Muffins

1½ cups flour

½ cup sugar

2 teaspoons baking powder

½ teaspoon salt

¼ cup vegetable oil

1 egg, beaten

1 cup milk

1 cup blueberries

Mix the flour, sugar, baking powder and salt together.

Blend the oil, egg and milk in a mixer bowl. Add the dry ingredients and mix just until moistened. Fold in the blueberries.

Spoon into greased and floured muffin cups. Bake at 350 to 400 degrees for 20 to 25 minutes or just until muffins begin to brown. Remove to a wire rack to cool.

❧ YIELDS 6 MUFFINS

Nut Bread

2 cups flour

¾ cup sugar

1 tablespoon baking powder

¼ teaspoon salt

1 cup chopped walnuts

2 eggs

1 cup milk

3 tablespoons melted butter

1 teaspoon vanilla extract

Sift the flour, sugar, baking powder and salt into a medium bowl. Stir in the walnuts.

Beat the eggs in a large mixer bowl until foamy. Stir in the milk, melted butter and vanilla. Add the flour mixture, stirring until smooth.

Spoon into a greased and floured loaf pan. Bake at 350 degrees for 50 to 55 minutes.

Cool in the pan on a wire rack for 10 minutes. Remove to the wire rack to cool completely.

❧ YIELDS 12 SERVINGS

Lemon Nut Bread

1/3 cup margarine, softened

1 cup sugar

1 tablespoon lemon extract

2 eggs

1 1/2 cups flour

1 teaspoon baking powder

1 teaspoon salt

1/2 cup milk

grated peel of 1 lemon

1/2 cup chopped pecans

1/3 cup fresh lemon juice

1/3 cup confectioners' sugar

Cream the margarine and sugar in a mixer bowl until light and fluffy.

Beat in the lemon extract. Beat in the eggs 1 at a time.

Add the flour, baking powder and salt alternately with the milk, mixing well after each addition.

Stir in the lemon peel and pecans.

Spoon into two 4x8-inch loaf pans sprayed with nonstick cooking spray.

Bake at 325 to 350 degrees for 30 minutes or until golden brown.

Blend the lemon juice and confectioners' sugar in a small bowl.

Spoon over the warm bread. Remove from the pans to a wire rack to cool.

Wrap the cooled loaves in waxed paper. Place in a sealable plastic bag and refrigerate for 24 hours before slicing.

Slice thin to serve.

❧ YIELDS 20 SERVINGS

Norwegian Bread

3½ cups flour

3 cups sugar

1 tablespoon baking soda

1 tablespoon cinnamon

1 teaspoon nutmeg

1½ teaspoons salt

1 cup vegetable oil

⅔ cup water

4 eggs, beaten

2 cups mashed cooked sweet
   potatoes

1 cup chopped pecans

Sift the flour, sugar, baking soda, cinnamon, nutmeg and salt into a bowl. Make a well in the center.

Add the oil, water, eggs, sweet potatoes and pecans to the well; mix until smooth.

Spoon into three 5x9-inch loaf pans. Bake at 350 degrees for 1 hour or until the loaves test done.

Cool in the pans for several minutes. Remove to a wire rack to cool completely.

❧ YIELDS 3 LOAVES

Coriander

Flat clusters of white to pale pink flowers on
this plant are followed by white, lemon-flavored seeds
that resemble peppercorns. The seeds are used
in curries, stir-fries and Scandinavian breads. The
leaves are referred to as cilantro and can be
used in salads, soups or salsa.

Irish Soda Bread

4 cups flour

1/2 cup sugar

1 tablespoon baking powder

1 teaspoon baking soda

1 teaspoon salt

1/2 cup butter, cut into chunks

1 1/4 cups buttermilk

1 egg

1 cup raisins

2 tablespoons caraway seeds

melted butter

sugar

Combine the flour, 1/2 cup sugar, baking powder, baking soda and salt in a large bowl. Cut in the butter until the mixture resembles fine crumbs.

Blend the buttermilk and egg in a small bowl. Add to the crumb mixture, stirring to form a soft dough. Mix in the raisins and caraway seeds.

Knead lightly on a floured surface 10 times or until smooth. Shape into a ball. Place on a baking sheet and press to flatten slightly. Make 2 slashes in the top to form a cross. Brush with melted butter and sprinkle with additional sugar.

Bake at 350 degrees for 50 to 60 minutes or until light brown. Remove to a wire rack to cool.

❧ YIELDS 12 SERVINGS

Caraway Seeds

Caraway seeds come from an herb in the parsley family. They are popular in European cooking, especially for breads, cakes, cheese and meats.

Meat
Chicken
Seafood

Everyone Needs Someone

People need people and friends need friends
And we all need love for a full life depends
Not on vast riches or great acclaim,
Not on success or on worldly fame,
But just in knowing that someone cares
And holds us close in their thoughts and prayers
For only the knowledge that we're understood
Makes everyday living feel WONDERFULLY GOOD,
And we rob ourselves of life's greatest need
When we "lock up our hearts" and fail to heed
The outstretching hand reaching to find
A kindred spirit whose heart and mind
Are lonely and longing to somehow share
Our joys and sorrows to make us aware
That life's completeness and richness depends
On the things we share with our loved ones and friends.

HELEN STEINER RICE

Easy Swiss Steak

1½ pounds sirloin or round
    steak

1 (10-ounce) can golden
    mushroom soup

1 (15-ounce) can stewed
    tomatoes, chopped

1 medium onion, sliced

¼ cup water

1 (4½-ounce) jar sliced
    mushrooms (optional)

salt and pepper to taste

Pound the steak with a meat mallet and cut into serving pieces.

Brown the steak in a nonstick skillet sprayed with nonstick cooking spray. Add the soup, tomatoes, onion, water, mushrooms, salt and pepper.

Simmer for 1¼ hours, stirring frequently.

❧ YIELDS 6 SERVINGS

Saucy Sirloin Surprise

1½ pounds sirloin steak, cut
    into 1-inch pieces

1 (10-ounce) can golden
    mushroom soup

¾ soup can water

chopped garlic to taste

1 bay leaf

2 tablespoons sherry

1 (10-ounce) package frozen
    green beans

Brown the steak in a nonstick skillet sprayed with nonstick cooking spray.

Add the soup, water, garlic, bay leaf and sherry. Simmer for 1 hour.

Add the beans. Simmer for 30 minutes longer or until tender; discard the bay leaf.

Serve over noodles or rice.

❧ YIELDS 4 TO 6 SERVINGS

Lobster–Stuffed Beef Tenderloin

1 (4- to 6-pound) beef
tenderloin, trimmed

3 lobster tails

1 tablespoon melted butter

garlic powder, salt and pepper
to taste

6 slices bacon

Butterfly the tenderloin lengthwise, cutting to but
not through the bottom and leaving ½ inch unsliced
at each end.

Place the lobster tails end-to-end along the cut,
slicing lengthwise if necessary to extend the entire
length of the tenderloin. Drizzle the lobster
with butter.

Tie the sides of the tenderloin together to enclose the
lobster, securing with string at 2- to 3-inch intervals.
Sprinkle with garlic powder, salt and pepper.

Place in a roasting pan and top with the bacon.
Insert a meat thermometer.

Roast at 400 degrees for 40 minutes or to
140 degrees for rare, or 160 degrees for medium.
Cut into 10 slices to serve.

Garnish with sprigs of fresh parsley.

❧ YIELDS 10 SERVINGS

Lavender

Lavender is a perennial shrub with graceful purple
flowers and a perfumelike scent that is more associated
with potpourri than cooking. However, its leaves and
flowers can be used in vinegar or jellies, and used
sparingly in salads, ice creams and custards. English
lavender is the hardiest of the species.

California Casserole

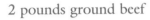

2 pounds ground beef

1 medium green bell pepper, chopped

3/4 cup chopped onion

1 (16-ounce) can cream-style corn

1 (10-ounce) can tomato sauce

1 (10-ounce) can tomato soup

1 (10-ounce) can tomatoes with green chiles

1 (4-ounce) can mushrooms

1 (2-ounce) can sliced black olives, drained

1 (4-ounce) jar chopped pimentos, drained

1/2 teaspoon chili powder

1/2 teaspoon dry mustard

1 1/2 teaspoons celery salt

1/4 teaspoon pepper

8 ounces wide egg noodles, cooked, drained

2 cups shredded Cheddar cheese

Brown the ground beef with the green pepper and onion in a Dutch oven, stirring until the ground beef is crumbly; drain.

Add the corn, tomato sauce, tomato soup, undrained tomatoes with green chiles, undrained mushrooms, olives, pimentos, chili powder, dry mustard, celery salt and pepper; mix well. Stir in the noodles.

Bake at 350 degrees for 50 minutes. Sprinkle with the cheese. Bake for 10 minutes longer or until the cheese melts.

❧ YIELDS 12 TO 16 SERVINGS

Chili

1 pound ground beef

1 large onion, chopped

1 green bell pepper, chopped

2 (16-ounce) cans kidney beans

2 cups chopped tomatoes

1 cup tomato sauce

1 to 1½ tablespoons chili powder

1 bay leaf

paprika and cayenne to taste

1½ teaspoons salt

Brown the ground beef with the onion and green pepper in a large saucepan, stirring until the ground beef is crumbly; drain.

Drain the beans, reserving the liquid. Add the beans, tomatoes, tomato sauce, chili powder, bay leaf, paprika, cayenne and salt to the ground beef mixture.

Simmer for 1½ hours, adding the reserved bean liquid and/or water as needed for the desired consistency. Discard the bay leaf before serving.

❧ YIELDS 4 SERVINGS

Red Flannel Hash

1 pound ground beef

½ cup chopped onion

1 (16-ounce) can pork and beans

½ cup catsup

2 tablespoons each sugar and vinegar

½ teaspoon each hot sauce and salt

¼ teaspoon pepper

Cook the ground beef with the onion in a saucepan, stirring until the ground beef is brown and crumbly and the onion is tender; drain.

Add the pork and beans, catsup, sugar, vinegar, hot sauce, salt and pepper.

Spoon into a 1½-quart baking dish. Bake at 375 degrees for 30 minutes.

❧ YIELDS 4 SERVINGS

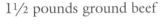

Prize-Winning Meat Loaf

1½ pounds ground beef

½ cup catsup

¾ cup quick-cooking oats

1 (10-ounce) can vegetarian
  vegetable soup

1 egg, beaten

1 teaspoon salt

¼ teaspoon pepper

Combine the ground beef, catsup, oats, soup, egg, salt and pepper in a bowl and mix well. Pack into a small loaf pan.

Bake at 350 degrees for 1 hour. Remove to a serving plate.

🐦 YIELDS 6 SERVINGS

Porcupines

1 pound ground beef

3 tablespoons chopped onion

¾ cup uncooked rice

¼ teaspoon poultry seasoning

1 teaspoon salt

¼ teaspoon pepper

2 (15-ounce) cans tomato
  sauce

1 cup water

Combine the ground beef, onion, rice, poultry seasoning, salt and pepper in a bowl and mix well. Shape into 12 balls.

Brown lightly on all sides in a covered saucepan; drain. Add the tomato sauce and water and mix well.

Simmer, covered, for 45 to 50 minutes or until the sauce is of the desired consistency.

🐦 YIELDS 4 SERVINGS

Baked Spaghetti

1 pound ground beef

1 cup chopped onion

1 cup chopped green bell pepper

1 tablespoon butter or margarine

1 (28-ounce) can chopped tomatoes

1 (4-ounce) can chopped mushrooms, drained

1 (2-ounce) can sliced black olives, drained

2 teaspoons dried oregano

12 ounces spaghetti, cooked, drained

2 cups shredded Cheddar cheese

1 (10-ounce) can cream of mushroom soup

1/4 cup water

1/4 cup grated Parmesan cheese

Brown the ground beef with the onion and green pepper in the butter in a large skillet, stirring until the ground beef is crumbly; drain.

Add the undrained tomatoes, mushrooms, olives and oregano. Simmer for 10 minutes.

Layer the spaghetti, ground beef mixture and Cheddar cheese 1/2 at a time in a 9x13-inch baking dish.

Mix the soup and water in a bowl. Pour over the layers. Sprinkle with the Parmesan cheese.

Bake at 350 degrees for 30 to 35 minutes or until bubbly.

Omit the ground beef for vegetarian spaghetti.

❧ YIELDS 12 SERVINGS

Chinese Spaghetti

1½ pounds ground beef

1 onion, chopped

¼ cup butter

1 (16-ounce) can meatless
    spaghetti in sauce

1 (15-ounce) can whole
    kernel corn, drained

1 (4-ounce) can mushrooms,
    drained

chow mein noodles

Brown the ground beef with the onion in the butter in a skillet, stirring until the ground beef is crumbly; remove from the heat and drain.

Stir in the spaghetti. Spoon into a baking dish.

Bake at 350 degrees for 40 minutes. Add the corn and mushrooms and mix well. Bake for 20 minutes longer.

Sprinkle noodles onto the serving plates. Spoon the spaghetti over the noodles and top with additional noodles. Serve with soy sauce.

YIELDS 6 SERVINGS

Marigold

Although all are edible, the Tangerine Gem and Lemon Gem varieties have a more pleasant flavor, and there is a Peruvian variety often used in salsa. Most marigolds are a good accompaniment to salads, soups and sauces and can be used as a substitute for saffron due to its taste and bright yellow coloring.

Golfers' Stew

2 to 3 pounds stew beef

1 medium onion, sliced

1 large clove of garlic, minced

1 cup chopped celery

3 or 4 carrots, chopped

1 (16-ounce) can tomatoes

1 tablespoon sugar

3 tablespoons quick-cooking
  tapioca

salt and pepper to taste

1 (8-ounce) can tomato sauce

1 (7-ounce) can water
  chestnuts, drained

1 (8-ounce) can sliced
  mushrooms, drained

Combine the beef, onion, garlic, celery, carrots, tomatoes, sugar, tapioca, salt and pepper in a 4-quart baking dish.

Add enough water to the tomato sauce to measure 1 cup. Stir into the baking dish.

Bake, covered, at 250 degrees for 4½ hours. Add the water chestnuts and mushrooms. Bake for 30 minutes longer.

You may substitute 8 ounces fresh mushrooms for the canned mushrooms and bake, uncovered, for 45 minutes.

❧ YIELDS 4 SERVINGS

Bouquet Garni

Tie a bundle of thyme, bay leaf, and lemon peel together. Added to soups and stews, it imparts a delightful flavor.

Santa Fe Stew

2 pounds ground beef or turkey

2 yellow onions, chopped

1 envelope ranch salad dressing mix

1 envelope taco seasoning mix

1 (15-ounce) can kidney beans

2 (15-ounce) cans pinto beans

2 (15-ounce) cans whole kernel corn

2 (15-ounce) cans diced tomatoes

2 (16-ounce) cans jalapeño black-eyed peas

Worcestershire sauce and Tabasco sauce to taste

salt and pepper to taste

3 cups shredded Cheddar cheese

Brown the ground beef with the onions in a large heavy saucepan, stirring until the ground beef is crumbly.

Add the salad dressing mix and taco seasoning mix. Stir in the undrained beans, corn, tomatoes and peas; mix well. Simmer, covered, for 20 minutes.

Remove from the heat and let stand for 10 minutes. Season with Worcestershire sauce, Tabasco sauce, salt and pepper.

Top servings with cheese.

❧ YIELDS 10 SERVINGS

Rosy Ham Loaf

1 pound ground cured ham

1 pound ground fresh pork

1 egg

1/2 cup catsup

1 cup milk

1 cup graham cracker crumbs

1/3 cup packed light brown
   sugar

1 tablespoon creamy
   horseradish sauce

1/2 cup sour cream

dash of Worcestershire sauce

Combine the ground ham, ground pork, egg,
catsup, milk and graham cracker crumbs in a bowl
and mix well.

Shape into a loaf in a 5x9-inch loaf pan. Sprinkle
with the brown sugar. Bake at 350 degrees for
1 hour. Remove to a serving plate.

Mix the horseradish sauce, sour cream and
Worcestershire sauce in a small bowl. Serve with
the ham loaf.

❧ YIELDS 8 SERVINGS

Baked Pork Chops

1 egg, beaten

1 cup half-and-half

salt and pepper to taste

6 (1-inch) boneless pork
   chops

seasoned bread crumb
   dressing mix

milk and cream

Mix the egg, half-and-half, salt and pepper in a
shallow dish. Add the pork chops and let stand for
several minutes. Coat with the dressing mix.

Arrange the pork chops in a baking dish sprayed with
nonstick cooking spray. Add enough milk and cream
to almost cover the pork chops.

Bake, covered with foil, at 325 degrees for 45
minutes. Add additional milk if needed to cover the
pork chops. Bake, covered, for 45 minutes longer,
removing the foil during the last 15 minutes of
baking time.

❧ YIELDS 6 SERVINGS

Dick Jones' Barbecued Pork

3 cups cider vinegar

1½ cups brown mustard or
  Dijon mustard

1 (5-pound) Boston butt

2 to 3 tablespoons Magnolia's
  Blackening Spice

Barbecue Sauce (page 59)

Mix the vinegar with the mustard in a bowl and set aside.

Rub the pork with the blackening spice. Place in a roasting pan and insert a meat thermometer into the thickest portion, not touching the bone.

Roast at 350 degrees for 1 hour. Reduce the oven temperature to 210 degrees. Roast the pork for 10 hours longer or to 190 degrees on the meat thermometer, basting every hour with the vinegar and mustard mixture. The pork should be tender enough to fall from the bone.

Toss shredded pork with Barbecue Sauce or serve the sauce on the side if desired.

❧ YIELDS 10 TO 12 SERVINGS

Magnolia's Blackening Spice

½ cup paprika

1 tablespoon each flour and
  chili powder

2 tablespoons garlic powder

1 tablespoon each onion
  powder, dried oregano,
  dried basil, dried thyme,
  cumin and salt

1 teaspoon black pepper

½ teaspoon cayenne

Combine the paprika, flour, chili powder, garlic powder, onion powder, oregano, basil, thyme, cumin, salt, black pepper and cayenne in a bowl and mix well.

Store in an airtight container for up to 6 months.

❧ YIELDS 1¼ CUPS

Barbecue Sauce

1½ cups cider vinegar

1 cup catsup

¼ cup Dijon mustard

2 tablespoons Worcestershire sauce

1 tablespoon Tabasco sauce

¼ cup black strap molasses

2 tablespoons dark brown sugar

1 teaspoon freshly ground pepper

Combine the vinegar, catsup, mustard, Worcestershire sauce, Tabasco sauce, molasses, brown sugar and pepper in a heavy saucepan.

Simmer over medium heat for 5 minutes or until the sauce is thick enough to coat a spoon.

Use at once or cool to room temperature. Store, covered, for several weeks in the refrigerator.

➤ YIELDS 2 CUPS

South Carolina Barbecue

Dick Jones gives credit for this barbecue to Magnolia's in Charleston, South Carolina. It is a great meal for picnics and family gatherings. The Blackening Spice can be used for any meat or even seafood. The Barbecue Sauce is a cross between a mopping sauce and a more traditional barbecue sauce. It can be used with pork or chicken, heated and tossed with the pulled meat, or served in a bowl on the side. You may add the pan drippings from any meat roasted in the oven if desired, but do not store for more than a week.

Highlands Pork Chops

4 (1-inch) pork chops

salt to taste

4 (¼-inch) onion slices

4 (¼-inch) tomato slices

4 (2-inch) green bell pepper
  slices

cooked rice

Brown the pork chops in a skillet over high heat for 5 minutes on each side. Remove to a 3-inch-deep baking dish and sprinkle with salt.

Place 1 onion slice and 1 tomato slice on each pork chop. Top with 1 green pepper ring and fill the ring with rice. Pour 1 to 2 inches water into the dish and cover tightly with foil.

Bake at 300 degrees for 3½ hours, basting after 1½ hours and taking care to baste the rice.

❧ YIELDS 4 SERVINGS

Thyme

The small, gray-green leaves have a sweet, savory flavor with an earthy aroma, while the lilac-colored flowers tend to be milder with a more floral scent, perfect for garnishing salads, pastas or desserts. This woody perennial has more than one hundred species and varieties, but most work well with a wide range of dishes.

Pork Chops with Honey-Mustard Sauce

¼ cup flour

½ teaspoon salt

¼ teaspoon pepper

4 (1-inch) pork chops, about 1½ to 2 pounds

1 tablespoon vegetable oil

1 large red bell pepper, cut into 1-inch pieces

2 large carrots, peeled, cut into ⅛x3-inch sticks

1½ cups low-sodium beef broth

1 tablespoon Dijon mustard

1 tablespoon honey

Mix the flour, salt and pepper in a bag. Add the pork chops and shake to coat well. Shake off excess flour; reserve the flour mixture.

Cook the pork chops in the heated oil in a medium skillet over medium heat for 8 minutes or until light brown on both sides. Remove to a serving plate.

Drain and wipe out the skillet, reserving 1 tablespoon of the drippings. Sauté the bell pepper and carrots in the reserved drippings for 5 minutes or until tender.

Stir in the reserved flour mixture. Cook for 1 minute or until brown, stirring constantly. Stir in the beef broth, mustard and honey. Cook for 1 to 2 minutes or until thickened, stirring constantly.

Add the pork chops and any juices. Simmer, covered, for 4 minutes or until the pork chops are cooked through. Serve with the sauce.

❧ YIELDS 4 SERVINGS

Bee Balm

Bees and hummingbirds are attracted to this citrus-tasting herb whose leaves and scarlet flowers can be used with fruits, duck and pork, or in salads, teas and jellies.

Oven-Roasted Chicken

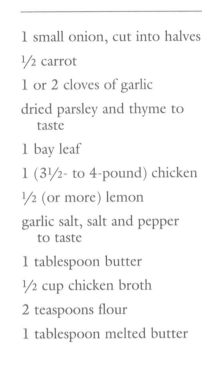

1 small onion, cut into halves

½ carrot

1 or 2 cloves of garlic

dried parsley and thyme to taste

1 bay leaf

1 (3½- to 4-pound) chicken

½ (or more) lemon

garlic salt, salt and pepper to taste

1 tablespoon butter

½ cup chicken broth

2 teaspoons flour

1 tablespoon melted butter

Place the onion, carrot, garlic, parsley, thyme and bay leaf in the chicken cavity. Squeeze the lemon juice over the outside and sprinkle with garlic salt, salt and pepper.

Place in an 8x8-inch roasting pan; dot with 1 tablespoon butter. Roast at 375 degrees for 1½ hours or until tender, basting every 15 minutes.

Remove the chicken to a serving plate and discard the bay leaf. Pour the chicken broth into the roasting pan, stirring to deglaze.

Blend the flour into the melted butter in a saucepan. Cook for 1 to 2 minutes, stirring constantly. Stir in the broth mixture gradually. Cook until thickened, stirring constantly. Serve with the chicken.

❧ YIELDS 6 SERVINGS

Sage

In ancient times the most common use of sage was for herbal teas, but today it generally seasons poultry stuffings and sausages. It can also be found in soups, omelets, rice, breads and vinegars, imparting a musky flavor with a hint of lemon. Harvest no more than the top third of this shrubby perennial with spikes of blue-violet flowers.

Microwave Juicy Chicken

1 (4-pound) chicken

seasoned salt

Place the chicken breast side down in a microwave-safe dish. Sprinkle with seasoned salt. Microwave on High for 18 minutes.

Turn the chicken breast side up and sprinkle with seasoned salt. Microwave on Medium-High for 18 minutes longer.

Let stand for 10 minutes before serving.

❧ YIELDS 4 OR 5 SERVINGS

Poppy Seed Chicken Casserole

1 (3-pound) chicken

2 cups sour cream

1 (10-ounce) can cream of mushroom soup

30 to 40 butter crackers, crushed

2 tablespoons poppy seeds

1/2 cup melted margarine

Cook the chicken in water to cover in a saucepan until tender. Cut into bite-size pieces, discarding the skin and bones. Combine with the sour cream and soup in a bowl and mix well.

Mix the cracker crumbs, poppy seeds and margarine in a medium bowl.

Layer half the crumb mixture, chicken mixture and remaining crumb mixture in a 2 1/2-quart baking dish.

Bake at 350 degrees for 30 to 40 minutes or until bubbly.

❧ YIELDS 8 SERVINGS

Apricot Chicken

1 chicken, cut up

salt to taste

1 cup French salad dressing

1 cup apricot preserves

½ cup water

Arrange the chicken in a 9x13-inch baking dish and sprinkle with salt.

Mix the salad dressing, preserves and water in a bowl. Spoon over the chicken.

Bake, covered with foil, at 350 degrees for 1 hour. Bake, uncovered, for 30 minutes longer.

❧ YIELDS 6 SERVINGS

Baked Chicken Breasts

4 boneless skinless chicken breasts

1 (10-ounce) can cream of mushroom soup

1 cup sour cream

¼ to ½ cup dry white wine

Arrange the chicken in a greased 2-quart baking dish. Combine the soup, sour cream and wine in a bowl and mix well. Spread over the chicken.

Bake at 350 degrees for 45 minutes or until tender. Serve over hot cooked white rice.

You may use reduced-fat soup and sour cream in the recipe.

❧ YIELDS 4 SERVINGS

Cheesy Chicken

12 boneless skinless chicken
  breasts

1 large onion, sliced into rings

2 (10-ounce) cans cream of
  mushroom soup

1/2 cup sherry

2 cups shredded sharp
  Cheddar cheese

paprika to taste

Arrange the chicken in a 9x13-inch baking dish.
Scatter the sliced onion over the top.

Mix the soup with the wine in a bowl. Pour over the
chicken. Sprinkle with the cheese and paprika.

Bake at 375 degrees for 1 1/2 hours. Serve over
noodles or rice.

~ YIELDS 12 SERVINGS

Chicken Cacciatore with Egg Noodles

1/4 cup flour

1 teaspoon dried Italian
  seasoning

1 (3- to 3 1/2-pound) chicken,
  cut up or quartered,
  skinned

2 tablespoons canola oil

2 (15-ounce) cans pasta-ready
  chunky tomatoes with
  olive oil and garlic

4 ounces egg noodles,
  cooked, drained

Mix the flour and Italian seasoning in a shallow dish.
Coat the chicken with the mixture.

Heat the oil in a large skillet over medium-high heat.
Add the chicken. Cook until golden brown on both
sides; drain the skillet and reduce the heat.

Add the undrained tomatoes to the skillet. Simmer,
covered, for 30 to 40 minutes or until the chicken is
tender and the juices run clear when the chicken is
pierced with a fork, stirring occasionally. Serve over
the noodles.

You may substitute chicken breasts for the cut-up
chicken.

~ YIELDS 4 SERVINGS

Chicken Cacciatore

3½ pounds cut-up chicken, skinned

¼ cup olive oil

2 small onions, thinly sliced, or 1 large

2 cloves of garlic, minced

⅓ cup tomato paste

¾ cup white wine or chicken broth

¾ cup chicken broth

¼ teaspoon thyme

¼ teaspoon marjoram

½ teaspoon basil

1 bay leaf

1 teaspoon salt

¼ teaspoon pepper

2 small tomatoes, seeded, chopped

4 ounces fresh mushrooms, sliced

1 large green bell pepper, cut into thin strips

Brown the chicken in the heated olive oil in a large skillet. Add the onions and garlic. Cook for several minutes, stirring constantly.

Combine the tomato paste, wine, chicken broth, thyme, marjoram, basil, bay leaf, salt and pepper in a small bowl; mix well. Add to the skillet. Simmer, covered, for 35 minutes, stirring occasionally.

Add the tomatoes, mushrooms and green pepper. Simmer, covered, for 20 minutes longer. Discard the bay leaf.

Serve with rice, rice pilaf or pasta.

❧ YIELDS 4 SERVINGS

Chicken Potpie

3 chicken breasts

1/2 cup margarine

1 (16-ounce) package frozen
mixed vegetables, thawed

1 (10-ounce) can cream of
chicken soup

1 cup baking mix

1 cup milk

1/2 cup melted margarine

Combine the chicken with 1/2 cup margarine and water to cover in a large saucepan. Cook until the chicken is tender; drain, reserving 1 cup broth. Chop the chicken into bite-size pieces, discarding the skin and bones.

Layer the chicken and vegetables in a 9x13-inch baking dish sprayed with nonstick cooking spray.

Mix the reserved broth with the soup in a bowl. Spread over the vegetables.

Combine the baking mix, milk and melted margarine in a bowl and mix until smooth. Spread over the layers.

Bake at 350 degrees for 45 minutes or until brown and bubbly.

❧ YIELDS 6 SERVINGS

Pizza Garden

Create your own pizza garden by planting the herbs you use in making pizza in a twelve-inch pot. This might include basil, thyme, marjoram, parsley and oregano. Snip as needed.

Chicken Spectacular

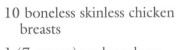

10 boneless skinless chicken breasts

1 (7-ounce) package long grain and wild rice mix

3 (16-ounce) cans French-style green beans, drained

1 (2-ounce) jar chopped pimento, drained

minced onion to taste

1 (7-ounce) can sliced water chestnuts, drained

1 cup mayonnaise

1 (10-ounce) can cream of celery, cream of chicken or cream of mushroom soup

salt and pepper to taste

1 (7-ounce) package herb dressing mix

Cook the chicken in water to cover in a saucepan until tender; drain. Cut into bite-size pieces.

Cook the rice using the package directions. Combine the chicken, rice, beans, pimento, onion and water chestnuts in a large bowl. Add the mayonnaise, soup, salt and pepper; mix gently.

Spoon into a 9x13-inch baking dish. Bake at 350 degrees for 30 minutes or until bubbly. Sprinkle with the dressing mix. Bake for 15 to 30 minutes longer or until golden brown.

Serve with fruit salad or aspic salad.

❧ YIELDS 10 TO 12 SERVINGS

Herbal Tea

To make herbal tea, heat the teapot with hot water. After you discard the water, place one teaspoon per cup of your favorite herb in the pot and add boiling water. Steep for five minutes. Strain into cups and enjoy!

Chicken Elegant

3 cups stuffing mix

6 boneless skinless chicken breasts

6 slices Swiss cheese

1 (10-ounce) can cream of chicken, cream of celery or cream of mushroom soup

1/2 cup sour cream

1/2 cup milk

1/2 cup water

Prepare the stuffing mix using the package directions. Arrange the chicken in an 8x12-inch baking dish. Arrange the cheese over the chicken.

Combine the soup, sour cream, milk and water in a saucepan and mix well. Cook until heated through. Pour gradually over the chicken.

Place a scoop of the stuffing on each piece of chicken.

Bake, covered, at 325 degrees for 1 1/2 hours.

❧ YIELDS 6 SERVINGS

Chicken Tetrazzini

1 green bell pepper, chopped

1 cup chopped celery

1 (10-ounce) can chicken broth

2 (10-ounce) cans cream of mushroom soup

2 to 3 cups chopped cooked chicken or turkey

1 (16-ounce) package spaghetti, cooked, rinsed, drained

1 to 2 cups shredded sharp cheese

Combine the green pepper and celery with the chicken broth in a saucepan. Cook until tender-crisp.

Stir in the soup. Add the chicken and spaghetti; mix gently.

Spoon into a greased 3-quart baking dish. Top with the cheese. Bake at 350 degrees until the tetrazinni is bubbly and the cheese melts.

You may add slivered almonds if desired.

❧ YIELDS 8 TO 10 SERVINGS

Company Chicken

1½ cups chopped cooked chicken

1 (7-ounce) can sliced water chestnuts, drained

1 cup chopped celery

½ cup toasted almonds

1 (10-ounce) can cream of celery soup

⅓ cup mayonnaise

salt and pepper to taste

1½ cups corn bread stuffing mix

6 tablespoons melted butter or margarine

Combine the chicken, water chestnuts, celery and almonds in a bowl. Add the soup, mayonnaise, salt and pepper; mix gently.

Spoon into an 8x8-inch baking dish. Bake at 350 degrees for 15 minutes.

Combine the stuffing mix with the melted butter in a bowl. Sprinkle over the casserole.

Bake for 15 to 20 minutes longer or until golden brown, checking during the last 8 to 10 minutes to prevent overbrowning.

You may use reduced-calorie mayonnaise and soup for this recipe.

❧ YIELDS 4 TO 6 SERVINGS

Hollyhocks

The flowers of hollyhocks are best used as an attractive container for a dish or as a garnish, but can also be made into fritters or flavoring for tea. They have spikes of single or double flowers of every color except true blue and have a very mild taste.

Fish with Peas and Potatoes in Paprika Sauce

4 fillets of monkfish or other firm white fish

1 teaspoon paprika

salt and freshly ground pepper to taste

1 pound small potatoes, sliced

4 small onions, sliced into rings

1 tablespoon chopped oregano

1 bay leaf

9 ounces fresh or frozen peas

4 cloves of garlic, sliced crosswise

1/3 cup olive oil

1 tablespoon white wine vinegar

1 teaspoon paprika

2 canned pimentos, sliced (optional)

Sprinkle the fish with 1 teaspoon paprika, salt and pepper; set aside.

Arrange the potatoes in a wide flameproof casserole. Top with the onions and sprinkle with the oregano. Add the bay leaf and water just to cover.

Bring to a boil over high heat; reduce the heat. Simmer for 15 minutes.

Add the peas and arrange the fish over the top. Simmer, covered, for 15 minutes or until the potatoes are tender. Drain, reserving 1/2 cup broth.

Sauté the garlic in the heated olive oil in a small saucepan just until light golden brown; remove from the heat.

Add the reserved broth, vinegar and 1 teaspoon paprika. Bring to a simmer. Pour over the casserole. Top with the pimentos.

Bake at 200 degrees for 5 to 10 minutes or just long enough to blend the flavors. Discard the bay leaf.

❧ YIELDS 4 SERVINGS

Salmon Bake

1 (16-ounce) can salmon, drained, flaked

1½ cups herb-seasoned stuffing mix

2 tablespoons finely chopped parsley

2 tablespoons finely chopped onion

3 eggs, beaten

1 (10-ounce) can cream of celery soup

Combine the salmon, stuffing mix, parsley, onion, eggs and soup in a bowl and mix well.

Spoon into a greased 1½-quart baking dish. Bake at 350 degrees for 50 minutes.

꙾ YIELDS 6 SERVINGS

Crab-Stuffed Flounder

2 tablespoons butter

2 teaspoons flour

1 teaspoon mustard

½ teaspoon Worcestershire sauce

3½ teaspoons lemon juice

salt and pepper to taste

⅔ cup milk

2 cups crab claw meat

1 (4-pound) flounder, boned, with pocket

Melt the butter in a saucepan. Stir in the flour, mustard, Worcestershire sauce, lemon juice, salt and pepper.

Add the milk gradually. Cook over low heat until thickened, stirring constantly. Stir in the crab meat.

Spoon the mixture into the pocket of the flounder; place in a shallow 10x15-inch baking dish.

Bake at 350 degrees for 25 minutes.

꙾ YIELDS 4 TO 6 SERVINGS

Christmas Flounder

Deviled Crab Supreme
(page 74)

1 pound shrimp, cooked,
peeled

1 (4- to 4½-pound) flounder,
cleaned, dressed for stuffing

4 large potatoes, sliced

2 large onions, sliced

8 slices bacon

1 cup water

Mix the deviled crab and shrimp in a bowl.

Place the flounder open on a work surface. Spoon the crab mixture onto the fish and arrange the potatoes and onions over the top. Replace the sides of the fish and place in an 11x15-inch baking dish.

Arrange the bacon over the fish. Add the water to the baking dish.

Bake at 350 degrees for 1 to 1½ hours or until the bacon is crisp and the fish flakes easily.

❧ YIELDS 8 SERVINGS

Christmas Flounder

During the Depression, people in southeastern North Carolina were forced to take advantage of "free" food rather than a purchased turkey for Christmas dinner. As a rule, a flounder was stuffed with other seafood and served with collards and grits at Christmas tables in the area—a tradition born of hardship and still remembered as part of the folklore of Lower Cape Fear.

Deviled Crab Supreme

3 slices bacon

2 ribs celery, minced

1 red onion, minced

1/2 green bell pepper, minced

1 pound crab meat

1/4 cup milk

1/3 cup mayonnaise

1 tablespoon catsup

1 teaspoon mustard

1 teaspoon Worcestershire
   sauce

3 drops of Tabasco sauce

1 slice bread, crumbled

Fry the bacon in a skillet until crisp. Remove and crumble the bacon; reserve the drippings in the skillet.

Add the celery, onion and green pepper to the drippings. Sauté until tender and the liquid is absorbed.

Combine the vegetables with the bacon, crab meat, milk, mayonnaise, catsup, mustard, Worcestershire sauce and Tabasco sauce in a bowl and mix well.

Spoon into ramekins; top with the bread crumbs. Bake at 350 degrees for 30 minutes.

You may use this mixture to stuff the Christmas Flounder (page 73).

❧ YIELDS 8 SERVINGS

Dill

Dill is an annual with finely divided green foliage and clusters of edible airy delicate yellow flowers that bloom from June to the first frost. Dill leaves flavor fish, vegetable dishes and salad dressing. Dill seed is generally used as a pickling spice and is harvested by hanging the flower stems upside down after seeds turn brown.

Deviled Crab

1 green bell pepper, finely
  chopped

1 onion, finely chopped

½ cup butter

¾ cup flour

1½ cups milk

1 egg

1 pound crab meat

2 tablespoons dry mustard

2 tablespoons Worcestershire
  sauce

dash of hot sauce

4 ounces crackers, crushed

paprika to taste

Sauté the green pepper and the onion in the butter in a saucepan. Stir in the flour. Cook for 1 minute, stirring constantly.

Stir in the milk gradually. Cook until thickened, stirring constantly. Stir a small amount of the hot mixture into the egg; stir the egg into the hot mixture. Cook for 1 minute, stirring constantly.

Add the crab meat, dry mustard, Worcestershire sauce and hot sauce. Reserve some of the cracker crumbs for topping. Stir the remaining crumbs into the crab mixture.

Spoon into baking shells. Top with the reserved cracker crumbs and paprika. Bake at 400 degrees for 20 minutes or until golden brown.

These may be frozen and baked at 200 degrees for several minutes before baking at 400 degrees as above.

❧ YIELDS 6 SERVINGS

Tarragon

The French variety of tarragon is a three-foot-tall woody perennial grown from cuttings and has narrow, dark green leaves and infrequent tiny, yellow flowers. It is best when used fresh and can flavor fish, chicken, vegetables or vinegar. Handle carefully when harvesting as they lose their oil when bruised.

Imperial Crab Casserole

½ green bell pepper, chopped

½ medium onion, chopped

2 ribs celery, chopped

1 pound crab meat

1 (2-ounce) jar chopped pimento

⅓ cup mayonnaise

1 tablespoon dry mustard

2 tablespoons seafood seasoning

Cook the green pepper, onion and celery in a small amount of water in a saucepan for 10 to 15 minutes or until tender; drain.

Combine the sautéed mixture with the crab meat, pimento, mayonnaise, dry mustard and seafood seasoning in a bowl and mix well.

Spoon into baking shells or a greased casserole. Bake at 400 degrees for 15 to 20 minutes or until bubbly.

❧ YIELDS 4 SERVINGS

Baked Crab and Shrimp

1 pound crab meat

1 pound peeled cooked small shrimp

½ cup chopped green onions with tops

½ cup chopped celery

1 cup mayonnaise

3 tablespoons Worcestershire sauce

1 tablespoon Tabasco sauce

¼ cup lemon juice

buttered bread crumbs

Combine the crab meat, shrimp, green onions, celery, mayonnaise, Worcestershire sauce, Tabasco sauce and lemon juice in a bowl; mix lightly to leave crab pieces as large as possible.

Spoon into a buttered baking dish. Top with the buttered bread crumbs.

Bake at 350 degrees for 25 to 30 minutes or until golden brown and bubbly.

❧ YIELDS 6 TO 8 SERVINGS

Crab Meat Soufflé

1 pound crab meat

1½ tablespoons
   Worcestershire sauce

1 tablespoon hot sauce

2 tablespoons lemon juice

½ cup mustard

½ cup mayonnaise

½ cup catsup

¼ cup melted butter

1 tablespoon paprika

2 egg yolks

½ cup hot milk

20 crackers, crushed

2 egg whites

Combine the crab meat, Worcestershire sauce, hot sauce, lemon juice, mustard, mayonnaise, catsup, butter, paprika and egg yolks in a bowl. Add the hot milk and cracker crumbs and mix well.

Beat the egg whites until stiff peaks form. Fold into the crab mixture.

Spoon into a round 2½-quart baking dish. Bake at 375 degrees for 30 minutes.

❧ YIELDS 8 SERVINGS

Marjoram

An aromatic herb of the mint family, the oval, velvety leaves of marjoram are good in soups, sauces and stuffings. The tiny pinkish-white flowers, also edible, bloom in midsummer and can be removed to increase leaf harvest. Sweet marjoram, the variety most often used in cooking, tastes like a milder, sweeter oregano.

Crab and Scallop Bake

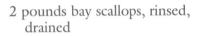

2 pounds bay scallops, rinsed, drained

1 (6-ounce) can crab meat, drained

1 cup chopped celery

1/4 cup chopped green bell pepper

2 to 3 tablespoons minced onion

1/2 teaspoon salt

pepper to taste

3/4 cup mayonnaise

1 teaspoon Worcestershire sauce

1 cup bread crumbs

2 tablespoons melted butter

Combine the scallops, crab meat, celery, green pepper, onion, salt and pepper in a bowl.

Mix the mayonnaise with the Worcestershire sauce in a small bowl. Add to the seafood mixture and mix well.

Spoon into a greased 2-quart baking dish. Toss the bread crumbs with the melted butter in a small bowl. Sprinkle over the casserole.

Bake at 350 degrees for 30 to 35 minutes or until the scallops are cooked through. Serve with rice.

❧ YIELDS 4 TO 6 SERVINGS

Parsley

Parsley is commonly used as a garnish. It may be eaten to freshen one's breath. Leaf infusions are used as a tonic for the hair and a skin freshener, or may be poured on cotton pads to place on tired eyes.

Scalloped Oysters

1 pint oysters

2 cups coarse cracker crumbs

1/2 cup melted butter

pepper to taste

3/4 cup light cream

1/4 teaspoon Worcestershire
    sauce

1/2 teaspoon salt

Drain the oysters, reserving 1/4 cup liquid.

Mix the cracker crumbs with the melted butter in a bowl. Spread 1/3 of the crumb mixture in a greased baking dish.

Layer half the oysters in the dish and sprinkle with pepper. Sprinkle with half the remaining crumbs and layer the remaining oysters over the top; sprinkle with pepper.

Combine the reserved oyster liquid, cream, Worcestershire sauce and salt in a bowl and mix well. Pour over the layers. Top with the remaining crumbs. Bake at 350 degrees for 40 minutes.

❧ YIELDS 4 SERVINGS

Shrimp Newburg

1 tablespoon flour

2 tablespoons melted butter

1 cup milk or light cream

2 hard-cooked eggs, grated

1/4 cup sherry

2 cups cooked shrimp

salt and pepper to taste

Blend the flour into the butter in a saucepan. Cook for 1 minute, stirring constantly.

Stir in the milk gradually. Cook until thickened, stirring constantly.

Add the eggs, wine, shrimp, salt and pepper. Cook just until heated through. Serve over rice.

❧ YIELDS 4 TO 6 SERVINGS

Garlic Shrimp with White Wine

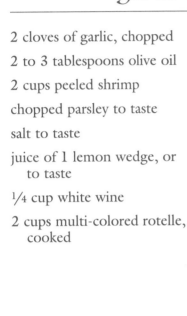

2 cloves of garlic, chopped

2 to 3 tablespoons olive oil

2 cups peeled shrimp

chopped parsley to taste

salt to taste

juice of 1 lemon wedge, or
   to taste

¼ cup white wine

2 cups multi-colored rotelle,
   cooked

Sauté the garlic lightly in the heated olive oil in
a skillet.

Add the shrimp, parsley, salt and lemon juice. Cook
until the shrimp begin to turn pink.

Add the wine. Cook, covered, for 2 to 3 minutes or
until the shrimp are cooked through.

Serve over the rotelle.

❧ YIELDS 4 SERVINGS

Garlic

Garlic lowers total cholesterol, inhibits blood clotting,
lowers blood pressure and reduces blood thickness. Try
the various forms of garlic: use flakes when you want
flavor and texture for casseroles and sauces; use granules
for flavor and thickening, but not texture; use powder
for flavor and aroma without texture, or as
thickening for sauces and salad dressings.

Vegetables
Side Dishes

A Volunteer's Prayer

I thank thee Lord, as a volunteer
For the chance to serve again this year;
To give of myself in some small way,
To those not blessed as I each day.
My thanks for health of mind and soul,
To aid me ever toward my goal;
For eyes to see the good in all,
A hand to extend before a fall.

For legs to go where the need is great,
Learning to love, forgetting to hate;
For ears to hear, and heart to care,
When someone's cross is hard to bear;
A smile to show my affection true,
With energy aplenty the risk to do;
And all I ask, dear Lord, if I may,
Is to serve you better, day by day.

Asparagus Casserole

1 (19-ounce) can asparagus
   spears

2 tablespoons cornstarch

1 tablespoon melted butter

3 tablespoons milk

1 (4-ounce) jar chopped
   pimentos, drained

2 hard-cooked eggs, sliced

3/4 cup shredded sharp
   Cheddar cheese

12 butter crackers, crushed

1 cup blanched slivered
   almonds

2 tablespoons melted butter

Drain the asparagus, reserving the liquid.

Blend the cornstarch with 1 tablespoon butter and the milk in a saucepan. Stir in the reserved asparagus liquid. Cook until thickened, stirring constantly.

Layer the asparagus, pimentos, eggs, cheese, cracker crumbs and sauce 1/2 at a time in a greased 6x10-inch baking dish. Top with the almonds. Drizzle with 2 tablespoons melted butter.

Bake at 400 degrees for 30 minutes.

❧ YIELDS 6 SERVINGS

Dandelion

A pesky perennial with a chicory taste when young
and tender, older dandelion leaves have a flavor similar
to spinach. Dandelion can be eaten fresh, cooked or
infused, and it blends well with garlic, tarragon,
chervil and burnet. The familiar yellow flower blooms
in May through July and can be minced and added
to butters, spreads and vinegar.

Asparagus Swiss Soufflé

½ cup chopped onion

¼ cup melted butter or margarine

½ cup flour

½ teaspoon salt

¼ teaspoon pepper

1 cup low-fat milk

1 cup shredded Swiss cheese

4 large egg yolks

4 large egg whites

Sauté the onion in the heated butter in a large saucepan over medium heat for 5 minutes.

Stir in the flour, salt and pepper. Cook for 2 minutes, stirring constantly.

Add the milk gradually. Cook for 5 minutes or until thickened, stirring constantly. Stir in the cheese until melted.

Whisk the egg yolks in a small bowl. Whisk in some of the hot cheese sauce; whisk the egg mixture into the hot sauce; remove from the heat. Fold in the asparagus.

Beat the egg whites in a mixer bowl until stiff peaks form. Fold in the asparagus mixture.

Spoon into a 1½-quart soufflé dish sprayed with nonstick cooking spray; place on a baking sheet.

Bake at 325 degrees for 50 minutes or until puffed and golden brown.

❧ YIELDS 8 SERVINGS

Barbecued Beans

8 ounces bacon

2 large onions, chopped

1 (10-ounce) package frozen
   baby lima beans

1 (16-ounce) can pork and
   beans, drained

1 (16-ounce) can red kidney
   beans

1 cup packed brown sugar

¼ cup vinegar

1 cup catsup

1 tablespoon mustard

1 tablespoon Worcestershire
   sauce

Cook the bacon in a skillet until crisp. Remove
and crumble the bacon, reserving the drippings in
the skillet.

Add the onions to the drippings and sauté until
tender; drain.

Cook the lima beans using the package directions for
15 minutes; drain.

Combine the lima beans with the pork and beans
and kidney beans in a bowl. Add the brown sugar,
vinegar, catsup, mustard, Worcestershire sauce,
sautéed onions and bacon and mix well.

Spoon into a 9x13-inch baking dish sprayed with
nonstick cooking spray. Bake at 350 degrees for
45 minutes.

You may substitute canned lima beans for the frozen
beans if preferred.

❧ YIELDS 8 TO 10 SERVINGS

Verbena

The lance-shaped leaves of this open-growing shrub are
the only lemon-scented foliage to retain its full scent
after drying. Its fresh or dried leaves can flavor
tea, fish, poultry, vegetable marinades, salad
dressings, jams and puddings.

Calico Beans

8 ounces bacon

8 ounces ground beef

1 large onion, chopped

½ cup packed brown sugar

½ cup catsup

2 tablespoons vinegar

1 tablespoon mustard

1 (16-ounce) can baked beans

1 (16-ounce) can lima beans, drained

1 (16-ounce) can butter beans, drained

1 (16-ounce) can kidney beans, drained

Cook the bacon in a skillet until crisp. Remove and crumble the bacon and drain the skillet.

Brown the ground beef with the onion in the skillet, stirring until the ground beef is crumbly; drain.

Add the brown sugar, catsup, vinegar and mustard to the ground beef and mix well. Simmer for 15 minutes.

Add the baked beans, lima beans, butter beans and kidney beans and mix well. Stir in the bacon.

Spoon into a large baking dish. Bake at 350 degrees for 45 minutes.

❧ YIELDS 10 TO 12 SERVINGS

Nasturtium

The slightly peppery taste of the young nasturtium leaves, flowers and buds combined with the vibrant oranges, reds or yellows of this annual brighten any green salad. The flowers also provide a unique container for cold salads, but the bitter-tasting base should be removed first.

Green Bean and Corn Casserole

1 (16-ounce) can French-style green beans, drained

1 (16-ounce) can Shoe Peg corn, drained

1/2 cup slivered almonds

1/2 cup finely chopped onion

1 (10-ounce) can cream of celery soup

1/2 cup sour cream

1/2 cup shredded Cheddar cheese

salt to taste

1 roll butter crackers, crushed

1/2 cup melted margarine

Combine the beans, corn and almonds in a greased rectangular baking dish.

Mix the onion, soup, sour cream, cheese and salt in a bowl. Spoon over the vegetable mixture.

Toss the cracker crumbs with the margarine in a bowl. Sprinkle over the casserole.

Bake at 350 degrees for 45 minutes.

❧ YIELDS 6 SERVINGS

Squash Blossoms

Golden-orange squash flowers begin to bloom in early summer and should be picked when fully open, but don't pick them all, or there will be no squash! The raw squash-flavored blossoms are usually stuffed and fried, but can also be chopped into soups, salads and vegetable dishes. Be sure to remove stamens and pistils before cooking.

Broccoli Casserole

2 (10-ounce) packages frozen chopped broccoli

1 (10-ounce) can cream of mushroom soup

1/2 cup mayonnaise

2 eggs, beaten

1/2 cup shredded Cheddar cheese

bread crumbs

butter or margarine

Cook the broccoli using the package directions; drain.

Combine the broccoli with the soup, mayonnaise, eggs and cheese in a bowl and mix well.

Spoon into a small baking dish. Sprinkle with bread crumbs and dot with butter.

Bake at 325 degrees for 30 minutes.

❧ YIELDS 6 SERVINGS

Broccoli and Corn Casserole

1 (16-ounce) package frozen chopped broccoli, thawed

1 (16-ounce) can cream-style corn

1/4 cup butter cracker crumbs

1 egg, beaten

1 tablespoon minced onion

1 teaspoon Mrs. Dash seasoning

1/2 cup butter cracker crumbs

2 tablespoons melted butter

Combine the broccoli, corn, 1/4 cup cracker crumbs, egg, onion and seasoning in a bowl and mix well. Spoon into a 1 1/2-quart baking dish.

Toss 1/2 cup cracker crumbs with the melted butter in a small bowl. Sprinkle over the casserole.

Bake at 350 degrees for 45 minutes.

❧ YIELDS 8 TO 10 SERVINGS

Broccoli with Noodles

1 (10-ounce) package frozen chopped broccoli

1 (8-ounce) package thin egg noodles

4 ounces fresh mushrooms, sliced

3 tablespoons butter

1 cup grated Parmesan cheese

5 tablespoons melted butter

Bring the broccoli to a boil in water to cover in a saucepan. Cook for 3 minutes. Drain the broccoli, reserving the cooking liquid; keep the broccoli warm.

Cook the noodles in the reserved liquid until tender.

Sauté the mushrooms in 3 tablespoons butter in a skillet until tender.

Drain the noodles and combine with the broccoli and mushrooms in a serving bowl. Add the cheese and 5 tablespoons butter; toss to mix well. Serve immediately.

❧ YIELDS 4 SERVINGS

Sesame Broccoli

2 pounds fresh broccoli, cut into 2-inch pieces

salt to taste

2 tablespoons vegetable oil

2 tablespoons vinegar

2 to 3 tablespoons Japanese soy sauce

2½ tablespoons sugar

2 tablespoons sesame seeds, toasted

Cook the broccoli in a small amount of salted boiling water in a saucepan just until tender-crisp; drain and keep warm.

Combine the oil, vinegar, soy sauce, sugar and sesame seeds in a small saucepan. Bring to a boil over medium heat, stirring to mix well.

Pour over the broccoli in a serving bowl and toss lightly. Serve immediately.

❧ YIELDS 6 SERVINGS

Baked Stuffed Eggplant

1 large eggplant

salt to taste

1 small onion, chopped

2 tablespoons butter

1 cup cooked shrimp

1 cup toasted bread crumbs

1 tablespoon lemon juice

1 egg yolk, beaten

2 tablespoons melted butter

Peel the eggplant and cut into halves lengthwise. Combine with salted water to cover in a saucepan. Cook for 10 minutes; drain.

Scoop the pulp from the eggplant, leaving ½-inch shells. Sprinkle the shells with salt and let stand. Cut the pulp into small pieces.

Sauté the onion in 2 tablespoons butter in a skillet. Add the shrimp, eggplant pulp, bread crumbs, lemon juice and egg yolk; mix well.

Spoon the mixture into the shells and place on a baking sheet. Sprinkle with additional bread crumbs and drizzle with the melted butter.

Bake at 375 degrees for 30 minutes.

❧ YIELDS 2 SERVINGS

Rosemary

Dark, gray-green leaves of rosemary resemble pine needles, and their faint minty taste has a pine undertone. Both the leaves and spiky pale blue flowers of this tender perennial are edible. It complements lamb, poultry, beef, vegetables and egg dishes.

Different Potato and Bean Casserole

2½ pounds new potatoes

turkey bacon or Canadian bacon

1 (20-ounce) can French-style green beans, drained

1 (10-ounce) can cream of chicken soup

1 cup sour cream

1 cup shredded Cheddar cheese

Cook the potatoes in water to cover in a saucepan until tender; drain and cut into cubes. Place in a 2½-quart baking dish.

Cook the bacon in a skillet until crisp; drain and crumble. Sprinkle the bacon over the potatoes. Layer the green beans over the bacon.

Combine the soup, sour cream and 1 cup cheese in a bowl and mix well. Spoon over the layers. Sprinkle with additional cheese.

Bake at 350 degrees for 30 to 45 minutes or until bubbly.

You may peel the potatoes or leave the skins on. Substitute light soup and sour cream if preferred.

YIELDS 6 SERVINGS

Rose

Older rose varieties seem to have more scent, therefore more taste, but many varieties can be quite bitter—so sample first. The hips, rich in vitamin C, and petals can be used for making tea, jelly, jam, syrup, or wine. The petals can also be candied or used to make rosewater, scented sugar or butter. Rose petals are also the main ingredient in potpourri.

Potato Casserole

1 (32-ounce) package frozen hash brown potatoes

1/2 cup melted margarine

1 cup sour cream

1 (10-ounce) can cream of chicken soup

1/2 cup chopped onion

2 cups shredded Cheddar cheese

1 teaspoon salt

1/2 teaspoon pepper

2 cups crushed corn flakes

1/2 cup melted margarine

Combine the potatoes, 1/2 cup margarine, sour cream, soup, onion, cheese, salt and pepper in a large bowl and mix well. Spoon into a greased 9x13-inch baking dish.

Mix the corn flake crumbs and 1/2 cup melted margarine in a small bowl. Sprinkle over the casserole.

Bake at 350 degrees for 40 to 45 minutes or until golden brown.

You may bake this in two 9-inch pie plates and adjust the baking time if preferred.

❧ YIELDS 12 SERVINGS

Daylily

The yellow, tawny orange flowers of all daylilies are edible, but sample first to determine taste before chopping into salads or soups. Pick the flower buds after they have elongated, but before they open, as the smaller buds tend to taste better. When sautéed, braised or stir-fried, they taste like a cross between asparagus and zucchini.

Spinach Casserole

2 eggs, beaten

6 tablespoons flour

1 (10-ounce) package frozen chopped spinach, thawed

1½ cups cottage cheese

1½ cups shredded Cheddar cheese

½ teaspoon salt

Beat the eggs with the flour in a bowl until smooth. Add the spinach, cottage cheese, Cheddar cheese and salt and mix well.

Spoon into a greased 1-quart baking dish. Bake at 350 degrees for 1 hour.

Serve as a vegetable or as a meatless main dish.

❧ YIELDS 4 TO 6 SERVINGS

Lemon Balm

Lemon balm is a perennial herb with a lemony flavor and a mint undertone. The fresh leaves can be used generously, whole or chopped, in salads, sauces and with poultry marinades. Its oil is used in furniture polish, and its fresh leaves can be rubbed on wooden surfaces for a similar result.

Squash Casserole

5 small yellow squash, sliced

salt to taste

1 small onion, chopped

1 carrot, shredded

1 rib celery, finely chopped

1 (10-ounce) can cream of chicken soup

1/2 cup sour cream

1 (8-ounce) package stove-top stuffing mix

1/4 cup water

1/2 cup melted margarine

1/2 cup shredded Cheddar cheese

Cook the squash in salted water to cover in a saucepan until tender; drain.

Combine the onion, carrot, celery, soup and sour cream in a bowl and mix well. Stir in the squash.

Combine the stuffing mix, water and margarine in a bowl. Sprinkle half the mixture in a buttered baking dish.

Spread the squash mixture in the prepared dish and sprinkle with the remaining stuffing mixture and cheese.

Bake at 350 degrees for 35 minutes.

You may also add cauliflower and/or broccoli if desired.

❧ YIELDS 8 SERVINGS

Cardamom

Cardamom is a spice with growing popularity. It is a pungent, sweet member of the ginger family with lemony undertones. Indians use it in curries, Middle Easterners use it in coffee, and Scandinavians bake with it. Try it to spice up a barbecue sauce, salad dressing or hot beverage.

Sweet Potato Casserole

3 cups mashed cooked sweet
  potatoes

1 cup sugar

1/2 cup melted butter

2 eggs, beaten

1/3 cup evaporated milk

1 teaspoon vanilla extract

1/2 cup packed brown sugar

1/4 cup flour

1/2 cup chopped pecans

2 1/2 teaspoons melted butter

Combine the sweet potatoes, sugar, 1/2 cup butter, eggs, evaporated milk and vanilla in a bowl and mix well. Spoon into a greased 8-inch baking dish.

Mix the brown sugar, flour, pecans and 2 1/2 teaspoons melted butter in a bowl. Sprinkle over the casserole.

Bake at 350 degrees for 25 minutes.

❧ YIELDS 6 TO 8 SERVINGS

Allium

Allium is a perennial herb that blooms during May and June with pretty lilac-pink flowers that, in addition to the hollow leaves, can be used as a garnish or as a substitute for scallions. It is a hardy plant that imparts an onion flavor to fish dishes, soups, salads, creamed cheeses or white vinegar.

Vegetable Casserole

2 (16-ounce) cans mixed
  vegetables, drained

1 (7-ounce) can water
  chestnuts, drained,
  chopped

1/2 cup chopped onion

1/2 cup mayonnaise

1 cup shredded cheese

1 roll butter crackers, crushed

1/2 cup melted margarine

Combine the vegetables, water chestnuts, onion, mayonnaise and cheese in a large bowl. Spoon into an 8x8-inch baking dish.

Mix the cracker crumbs and margarine in a small bowl. Sprinkle over the casserole.

Bake at 350 degrees for 25 minutes.

❧ YIELDS 6 TO 8 SERVINGS

Fettuccini Alfredo

16 ounces uncooked
  fettuccini

1 cup butter

1 to 2 tablespoons chopped
  parsley

1 1/2 cups grated Parmesan
  cheese

Cook the pasta in boiling water in a large saucepan for 5 minutes or until tender; drain.

Melt the butter in a large skillet over medium heat; remove from the heat. Stir in the parsley. Add the pasta and cheese; toss to coat well.

Serve immediately with additional Parmesan cheese.

❧ YIELDS 6 TO 8 SERVINGS

Macaroni with Four Cheeses

16 ounces elbow macaroni

3 tablespoons butter

1 onion, finely chopped

1 clove of garlic, minced

3 tablespoons flour

3 cups hot skim milk

1¾ cups shredded sharp
    Cheddar cheese

¼ cup grated Parmesan
    cheese

1 cup shredded Gruyère or
    Swiss cheese

½ cup crumbled bleu cheese

½ teaspoon dry mustard

6 drops of red pepper sauce

½ teaspoon salt

⅛ teaspoon pepper

4 plum tomatoes, peeled,
    seeded, chopped

1 cup fresh bread crumbs

1 tablespoon chopped parsley

¼ cup each shredded sharp
    Cheddar cheese and grated
    Parmesan cheese

2 tablespoons melted butter

Cook the macaroni al dente using the package directions; drain, rinse with cold water and drain again.

Melt 3 tablespoons butter in a medium saucepan over medium heat. Add the onion and garlic and sauté for 4 minutes. Stir in the flour. Cook for 1 minute. Whisk in the hot milk gradually. Cook for 1 minute or until thickened, stirring constantly; remove from the heat.

Add 1¾ cups Cheddar cheese, ¼ cup Parmesan cheese, Gruyère cheese, bleu cheese, dry mustard, pepper sauce, salt and pepper; stir until the cheeses melt. Combine with the macaroni and tomatoes in a bowl and mix gently.

Spoon into a greased 9x13-inch baking dish. Bake at 375 degrees for 15 minutes.

Combine the bread crumbs with the parsley, ¼ cup Cheddar cheese and ¼ cup Parmesan cheese in a bowl. Add 2 tablespoons melted butter and mix well. Sprinkle over the macaroni.

Bake for 10 to 15 minutes longer or until golden brown and bubbly.

You may use the cheese and pasta of your choice or substitute margarine for the butter in this recipe.

❧ YIELDS 8 SERVINGS

Ziti with Vegetables and Feta Cheese

8 ounces uncooked ziti

olive oil

3 medium tomatoes, cut into wedges

6 to 8 mushrooms, sliced

1 small onion, chopped

1 tablespoon olive oil

8 to 10 (1/2-inch) slices roasted red bell pepper

1/2 cup water

1/4 cup wine

1 tablespoon tomato paste

1 bouillon cube (optional)

1 teaspoon minced garlic

1 teaspoon dried basil

8 ounces feta cheese, crumbled

Cook the ziti using the package directions. Drain the pasta, drizzle with olive oil and keep warm.

Sauté the tomatoes, mushrooms and onion in 1 tablespoon olive oil in a large skillet for 5 minutes.

Add the red bell pepper, water, wine, tomato paste, bouillon cube, garlic and basil and mix well. Simmer, loosely covered, for 10 minutes or until of the desired consistency.

Spoon the pasta onto the serving plates. Spoon the sauce over the top. Sprinkle with the cheese.

Serve with salad or a steamed vegetable and Italian bread.

❧ YIELDS 3 OR 4 SERVINGS

Lilac

The pyramidal lavender clusters of lilac flowers are known for their scent, which carries over into their taste. Lilac can be candied or used in fritters, herb butters, scented sugars or as a garnish. They blossom in late spring and should be picked as soon as they open.

Carolina Red Rice

4 ounces bacon

¾ cup chopped onion

2 cups uncooked rice

2 cups canned tomatoes

¼ teaspoon Tabasco sauce

½ teaspoon salt

½ teaspoon pepper

Cook the bacon in a skillet until crisp. Remove and crumble the bacon, reserving the drippings in the skillet.

Add the onion to the drippings and cook until tender. Add the rice, tomatoes, bacon, Tabasco sauce, salt and pepper.

Cook over low heat for 35 minutes, stirring frequently and adding water after 15 minutes if needed.

❧ YIELDS 6 SERVINGS

Mediterranean Rice Pilaf

3 cups chicken broth

1½ cups uncooked long grain rice

⅔ cup seedless golden raisins

½ teaspoon olive oil

3 tablespoons soy sauce

½ teaspoon curry powder

½ teaspoon turmeric

Bring the chicken broth to a boil in a medium saucepan. Stir in the rice, raisins, olive oil, soy sauce, curry powder and turmeric.

Simmer, covered, for 20 minutes or until the rice is tender and the liquid is absorbed.

❧ YIELDS 8 SERVINGS

Baked Pineapple

6 tablespoons flour

1/2 cup sugar

2 (15-ounce) cans pineapple chunks, drained

2 cups shredded sharp cheese

1 cup fine cracker crumbs

1/2 cup melted margarine

Mix the flour and sugar in a bowl. Add the pineapple and toss to mix well. Add the cheese.

Spoon into a 1-quart baking dish. Sprinkle with cracker crumbs and drizzle with margarine.

Bake at 375 degrees for 45 minutes. Serve hot or at room temperature.

❧ YIELDS 8 SERVINGS

Pineapple Soufflé

1 (20-ounce) can crushed pineapple

3 tablespoons flour

3 eggs

2 tablespoons melted butter

2 tablespoons sugar

juice of 1 lemon

1 teaspoon salt

Drain the pineapple, reserving the juice. Blend the flour into the reserved juice in a bowl.

Add the pineapple, eggs, butter, sugar, lemon juice and salt and mix well. Spoon into a 1 1/2-quart baking dish.

Bake at 350 degrees for 40 to 50 minutes or until bubbly.

❧ YIELDS 4 SERVINGS

Apple and Cranberry Casserole

3 cups chopped unpeeled red
 apples

2 cups whole cranberries

1 to 1½ cups sugar

1 cup rolled oats

½ cup packed brown sugar

⅓ cup flour

½ cup chopped pecans

½ cup margarine

Toss the apples and cranberries with the sugar in a bowl. Place in a deep round baking dish.

Mix the oats, brown sugar, flour and pecans in a bowl. Sprinkle over the fruit mixture; dot with the margarine.

Bake, covered, at 350 degrees for 50 minutes. Bake, uncovered, for 10 minutes longer.

❧ YIELDS 6 TO 8 SERVINGS

Storing Herbs

Store dried herbs and spices in a cool dark
place to retain flavor and color. Never store them
in a place where the temperature fluctuates,
such as near the kitchen range.

Apple and Cranberry Relish

1¼ cups sugar

1 cup water

1 tablespoon finely chopped
orange peel

1½ pounds Granny Smith
apples, peeled, chopped

1 (10-ounce) package
cranberries, coarsely
chopped

1 tablespoon finely chopped
crystallized ginger, or
¼ teaspoon ground

¼ teaspoon ground allspice

¼ teaspoon ground
cinnamon

½ cup raisins

Combine the sugar, water and orange peel in a heavy medium saucepan. Bring to a boil and reduce the heat. Simmer for 2 minutes, stirring to dissolve the sugar.

Add the apples. Simmer for 5 minutes, stirring constantly.

Add the cranberries, ginger, allspice and cinnamon. Simmer for 7 to 8 minutes or until the cranberries are tender, stirring constantly. Stir in the raisins.

Spoon into a serving bowl and let cool. Chill for 8 hours or longer.

You may store this relish in sterilized jars in the refrigerator for up to 2 weeks.

Serve in place of cranberry sauce, as a relish on sandwiches or even on ice cream.

❧ YIELDS 5 TO 6 CUPS

Gingerroot

Preserve leftover fresh gingerroot by peeling it and placing it in a jar. Cover with dry sherry and store, covered. Use as you would fresh ginger.

Freezer Pickles

6 cups sliced cucumbers

1 cup sliced white onion

1 cup chopped green bell
    pepper

2 cups sugar

1 cup white vinegar

1 teaspoon pickling spice

1 tablespoon salt

Combine the cucumbers, onion and green pepper in a large bowl.

Mix the sugar, vinegar, pickling spice and salt in a small bowl until the sugar dissolves.

Add to the cucumber mixture and mix well. Chill in the refrigerator for 8 hours or longer.

Spoon into freezer containers. Store in the freezer. Let stand at room temperature for several hours before serving.

❧ YIELDS 6 TO 7 CUPS

Basil

The leaf harvest of basil is increased if the leaves are picked before the white-pale pink flowers open. After the leaves are picked, they should be kept in an airtight container—unwashed, as water blackens the leaves. Basil can be used on pizza or with a variety of meats, fowl and vegetables. Combined with butter, vinegar or oil, it imparts a sweet flavor with a suggestion of mint and clove.

Cakes
Cookies

A Toast to Hospital Volunteers

Lift your glasses, give a loud cheer
Help us to honor a hospital volunteer!
In the community, wherever people are
She helps the hospital with its PR.
She serves mankind in wise gentle ways
She warms patients' hearts and brightens their days.
She's a health care angel who walks on earth
And hereby we wish to acknowledge her worth.
So for this tribute we all stand to say,
"It's sure good to know you! Hip, Hip, Hooray!"

AND FURTHERMORE

The men have joined in the work we do
They're wise, thoughtful, strong and true.
They, too, are angels whose efforts don't cease
May their influence be felt and their numbers increase!

FRAN BENNETT

Apple and Raisin Cake

2 cups sugar

2 eggs

1½ cups vegetable oil

3 cups flour

1 teaspoon baking soda

1 teaspoon cinnamon

½ teaspoon salt

3 cups chopped apples

¾ cup raisins or cherries

½ cup chopped pecans

¾ cup shredded coconut

2 teaspoons vanilla extract

½ cup packed brown sugar

½ cup melted margarine

½ cup milk

Beat the sugar with the eggs until thick and pale yellow. Beat in the oil.

Sift the flour, baking soda, cinnamon and salt together. Add to the egg mixture and mix well. Stir in the apples, raisins, pecans, coconut and vanilla.

Spoon into a greased and floured tube pan. Bake at 300 degrees for 1 hour. Cool in the pan for several minutes. Remove to a wire rack to cool completely. Place on a serving plate.

Combine the brown sugar, margarine and milk in a small bowl and mix well. Spoon over the cooled cake.

❧ YIELDS 16 SERVINGS

Cinnamon

Cinnamon is the inner bark of a tropical evergreen and is sold as sticks or ground into powder. Its pungent, slightly bittersweet flavor is widely used in sweet dishes, but also enhances savory soups and stews.

Apple Cake

2 eggs

4 cups sliced apples

2 cups sugar

1/2 cup light vegetable oil

2 cups flour

3/4 teaspoon baking powder

2 teaspoons each baking soda
   and cinnamon

3/4 teaspoon salt

1 teaspoon vanilla extract

1 cup chopped nuts

Add the eggs to the apples in a bowl and mix with a fork. Add the sugar and oil and mix well.

Mix the flour, baking powder, baking soda, cinnamon and salt together. Add to the apples and mix well. Stir in the vanilla and nuts.

Spoon into a 9x13-inch baking pan. Bake at 325 degrees for 1 hour.

❧ YIELDS 15 SERVINGS

Easy Coconut Cake

1 (2-layer) package white cake
   mix

2 cups sour cream

2 cups confectioners' sugar

2 (8-ounce) packages frozen
   shredded coconut, thawed

9 ounces whipped topping

Prepare and bake the cake mix using the package directions for 2 layers. Split the cooled layers horizontally into 4 layers.

Mix the sour cream, confectioners' sugar and coconut in a bowl. Reserve 1/2 cup of the coconut mixture. Spread the remaining coconut mixture between the cake layers.

Combine the reserved coconut mixture with the whipped topping. Spread over the top and side of the cake. Chill in the refrigerator for 3 days if possible to improve the flavor.

❧ YIELDS 16 SERVINGS

Blackberry Wine Cake

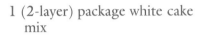

1 (2-layer) package white cake mix

1 (3-ounce) package blackberry gelatin

4 eggs

1/2 cup vegetable oil

1 cup blackberry wine

1/2 cup chopped pecans

1 cup confectioners' sugar

1/4 cup margarine

1/3 cup blackberry wine

Combine the cake mix and gelatin in a mixer bowl. Add the eggs, oil and 1 cup blackberry wine.

Beat at low speed until moistened. Beat at medium speed for 2 minutes, scraping the side of the bowl frequently.

Sprinkle the pecans into a greased and floured bundt pan. Spoon the batter into the prepared pan.

Bake at 350 degrees for 45 to 50 minutes or until the cake tests done. Cool in the pan for 25 minutes. Remove to a serving plate.

Combine the confectioners' sugar, margarine and 1/3 cup blackberry wine in a saucepan. Bring to a boil, stirring to mix well; remove from the heat. Cool slightly. Pour over the cake.

Let stand for 8 hours before serving.

❧ YIELDS 16 SERVINGS

Sweet Woodruff

A staple of the May wine punch bowl, the tiny star-shaped white flowers of this shade-loving perennial can also be seen garnishing tea cakes, desserts, salads and fruits, especially berries. The scent of its bright green leaves, a cross between new-mown hay and vanilla, is released when they are dried.

Franklin Nut Cake

2 cups butter, softened

2 cups sugar

6 eggs

2 teaspoons vanilla extract

4 cups flour

1 teaspoon baking powder

¼ teaspoon salt

8 ounces red candied cherries, chopped

8 ounces green candied cherries, chopped

8 ounces candied pineapple, chopped

1 pound pecans, chopped

Cream the butter and sugar in a mixer bowl until light and fluffy. Beat in the eggs and vanilla.

Sift the flour, baking powder and salt together. Add 3 cups of the mixture to the creamed mixture and mix well.

Toss the cherries, pineapple and pecans with the remaining flour mixture. Fold into the batter.

Spoon into a greased and floured tube pan. Bake at 250 degrees for 2½ to 3 hours or until a wooden pick inserted near the center comes out clean.

Cool in the pan for several minutes. Remove to a wire rack to cool completely.

❧ YIELDS 16 SERVINGS

Pineapple Sage

Rough, dark green leaves and bright scarlet tubular flowers, that bloom in late summer, characterize this tender perennial, which can be brought indoors during the winter. The flowery, pineapple taste, with a hint of sage muskiness, lends itself to seasoning fruit salads, tea, desserts, and tea breads.

"Hi, Buddy" Butter Fruitcake

2 (8-ounce) jars maraschino
  cherries

½ cup Port

3 cups each candied pineapple
  and cherries

4 cups each golden or dark
  raisins and chopped pecans

3 cups chopped black walnuts

1½ cups butter, softened

1½ cups sugar

8 eggs

2½ cups flour

1 teaspoon salt

Drain the maraschino cherries, reserving the juice. Combine the reserved juice with the wine in a bowl. Add the candied pineapple, candied cherries, raisins, pecans and walnuts. Let stand for 8 hours or longer.

Cream the butter and sugar in a mixer bowl until light and fluffy. Beat in half the eggs. Add the flour and salt and mix well. Beat in the remaining 4 eggs.

Fold in the undrained soaked fruit and the cherries. Spoon into a greased and floured bundt pan. Bake at 280 degrees for 4 hours. Cool in the pan for several minutes. Remove to a wire rack to cool completely.

You may add some brandy or rum to the soaking fruit if desired. This recipe may also be baked in 2 loaf pans, filling ¾ full.

❧ YIELDS 20 SERVINGS

A Volunteer Buddy

The recipe for "Hi, Buddy" Butter Fruitcake came originally from J.E.L. (Jimmy) Wade, one of Wilmington's most colorful characters. He was famous for greeting everyone with the expression, "Hi, Buddy." While serving as the mayor of Wilmington, he was responsible for sponsoring the World's Largest Living Christmas Tree. He gave more than a "pinch of time" in his volunteer work at the U.S.O. and in playing Santa Claus for countless numbers of children.

Fruitcakes

2 pounds candied cherries

2 pounds candied pineapple

1 pound seedless raisins

8 ounces fresh or frozen
   grated coconut

2 pounds pecans

1 cup flour

1½ pounds butter, softened

4½ cups sugar

9 eggs

5 cups flour

1 (8-ounce) can crushed
   pineapple

1½ teaspoons baking powder

2 teaspoons apple brandy

sweet wine

Combine the candied cherries, candied pineapple, raisins, coconut and pecans in a large bowl. Add 1 cup flour and toss to coat well.

Cream the butter and sugar in a mixer bowl until light and fluffy. Beat in the eggs 1 at a time.

Add 5 cups flour alternately with the crushed pineapple and baking powder, mixing well after each addition. Add the fruit and apple brandy and mix gently.

Line two 9-inch tube pans with greased baking parchment. Spoon the batter into the prepared pans. Place in an oven preheated to 225 degrees and place a shallow pan of water on the lower rack.

Bake for 3 to 4 hours or until wooden picks inserted into the centers come out clean. Cool in the pans for 45 to 60 minutes. Remove from the pans.

Drizzle with wine and wrap well with foil. Let stand for 3 to 4 days. Freeze for 2 weeks.

Thaw cakes and pierce with an ice pick. Drizzle with wine and store in the refrigerator or a cool place.

🍂 YIELDS 2 LARGE CAKES

Hawaiian Wedding Cake

1 (2-layer) package yellow or white cake mix

1 (4-ounce) package vanilla instant pudding mix

1 cup milk

8 ounces cream cheese

1 (20-ounce) can crushed pineapple, drained

8 ounces whipped topping

1 cup shredded coconut

1/2 cup chopped nuts

Prepare and bake the cake using the package directions for a 9x13-inch cake pan. Cool to room temperature.

Combine the pudding mix, milk and softened cream cheese in a bowl and mix until smooth. Fold in the pineapple. Spread on the cake.

Spread the whipped topping over the pineapple mixture; sprinkle with coconut and nuts.

You may use light cake mix, skim milk, light cream cheese and light whipped topping in this recipe.

❧ YIELDS 15 SERVINGS

Honey Bun Cake

1 (2-layer) package yellow cake mix

1 cup buttermilk

4 eggs

3/4 cup vegetable oil

1 cup packed brown sugar

4 teaspoons cinnamon

1/2 cup chopped nuts

1 cup confectioners' sugar

3 tablespoons milk

1 teaspoon vanilla extract

Combine the cake mix, buttermilk, eggs and oil in a bowl and mix by hand or with a mixer for 1 minute. Spoon into a greased and floured tube pan.

Combine the brown sugar, cinnamon and nuts in a small bowl. Sprinkle over the batter and cut in with several strokes of a knife. Bake at 300 degrees for 1 hour. Remove to a serving plate.

Mix the confectioners' sugar, milk and vanilla in a small bowl. Drizzle over the hot cake.

❧ YIELDS 16 SERVINGS

Honey Spice Chiffon Cake

2 cups flour

1¼ cups sugar

1 tablespoon baking powder

1 teaspoon salt

1 cup vegetable oil

7 egg yolks, slightly beaten

¾ cup cold water

1 teaspoon cinnamon

½ teaspoon each nutmeg,
 allspice and cloves

1 cup egg whites

½ teaspoon cream of tartar

Brown Sugar Frosting

chopped walnuts

Sift the flour, sugar, baking powder and salt into a large bowl; make a well in the center.

Add the oil, egg yolks, cold water, cinnamon, nutmeg, allspice and cloves to the well. Beat by hand or with a mixer until smooth.

Beat the egg whites with the cream of tartar in a mixer bowl until stiff peaks form. Pour the batter gradually over the egg whites, folding in gently.

Spoon into an ungreased 10-inch tube pan. Bake at 325 degrees for 55 to 60 minutes or until a knife inserted near the center comes out clean.

Invert the pan and let cool for 2 hours. Remove to a serving plate.

Spread the Brown Sugar Frosting over the cake; sprinkle with walnuts.

❧ YIELDS 16 SERVINGS

Brown Sugar Frosting

½ cup butter

2½ tablespoons flour

¼ teaspoon salt

½ cup milk

1½ cups packed light brown
 sugar

1 cup sifted confectioners'
 sugar

1 teaspoon vanilla extract

Melt the butter in a saucepan. Blend in the flour and salt. Cook until bubbly, stirring frequently.

Add the milk. Cook for 1 minute or until thickened, stirring constantly. Stir in the brown sugar; remove from the heat.

Add the confectioners' sugar and vanilla. Beat until of spreading consistency.

❧ FROSTS 1 CAKE

Hummingbird Cake

1 (8-ounce) can crushed
  pineapple

1 (2-layer) package yellow
  cake mix

1 (4-ounce) package vanilla
  instant pudding mix

½ cup vegetable oil

4 eggs

1 teaspoon cinnamon or apple
  pie spice

½ tablespoon almond extract

¼ cup chopped drained
  maraschino cherries

½ cup finely chopped pecans

Cream Cheese and Pecan
  Frosting

Drain the pineapple, reserving the juice. Mix the
reserved juice with enough water to measure 1 cup.

Combine the cake mix and pudding mix in a mixer
bowl. Add the oil, pineapple, pineapple juice
mixture, eggs, cinnamon and almond extract; mix
until moistened. Beat at medium speed for 2
minutes. Stir in the cherries and pecans.

Spoon into a 10x15-inch cake pan. Bake at 350
degrees for 50 minutes or until a wooden pick
inserted in the center comes out clean. Cool on a
wire rack.

Spread with Cream Cheese and Pecan Frosting.

❧ YIELDS 15 SERVINGS

Cream Cheese and Pecan Frosting

8 ounces cream cheese,
  softened

6 tablespoons butter, softened

1 (1-pound) package
  confectioners' sugar

1 cup chopped pecans

Beat the cream cheese and butter in a mixer bowl
until light.

Add the confectioners' sugar and beat until smooth.
Stir in the pecans.

❧ FROSTS 1 CAKE

Key Lime Cake

½ cup unsalted butter,
softened

1 cup sugar

2 eggs

1¾ cups flour

2 teaspoons baking powder

½ teaspoon salt

⅔ cup heavy cream

grated peel of 1 Key lime

1 tablespoon Key lime juice

1 cup confectioners' sugar,
sifted

½ cup Key lime juice

3 tablespoons confectioners'
sugar

1 cup sweetened whipped
cream

Cream the butter in a mixer bowl until light. Add the sugar gradually, beating until fluffy. Beat in the eggs 1 at a time.

Sift the flour, baking powder and salt together. Add to the creamed mixture alternately with the cream, beginning and ending with the flour mixture and mixing well after each addition. Stir in the lime peel and 1 tablespoon lime juice.

Spoon into a greased 6-cup bundt pan. Bake at 350 degrees for 50 minutes. Remove to a serving plate.

Blend 1 cup confectioners' sugar with ½ cup lime juice. Drizzle gradually over the warm cake until the mixture is absorbed.

Sift 3 tablespoons confectioners' sugar over the top. Serve with the whipped cream.

❧ YIELDS 10 SERVINGS

Melt-in-Your-Mouth Lemon Loaf Cakes

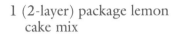

1 (2-layer) package lemon
  cake mix

1 (4-ounce) package lemon
  pudding mix

1 cup boiling water

½ cup vegetable oil

4 eggs, slightly beaten

1 cup confectioners' sugar

6 tablespoons fresh lemon
  juice

1 tablespoon melted
  margarine

Combine the cake mix, pudding mix, boiling water, oil and eggs in a mixer bowl. Beat for 5 minutes.

Spoon into 2 greased and floured loaf pans. Bake at 350 degrees for 45 minutes.

Combine the confectioners' sugar, lemon juice and margarine in a bowl and mix well.

Punch holes in the warm cakes. Drizzle with the glaze. Let stand until cool.

🐦 YIELDS 20 SERVINGS

Honeysuckle

Many are familiar with this fairly invasive-growing perennial, known for its delightful fragrance and sweet honey taste. Honeysuckle can be used in puddings, ice creams or syrups. The flowers are creamy white, yellow, pink or red in color and bloom from May to July.

Orange Poppy Seed Cake

2 tablespoons poppy seeds

1/4 cup milk

3 cups cake flour

2 1/2 teaspoons baking powder

1/4 teaspoon salt

1 1/4 cups unsalted butter, softened

1 3/4 cups sugar

4 eggs

1 tablespoon finely grated orange peel

2 teaspoons vanilla extract

3/4 cup orange juice

1 cup confectioners' sugar

1 teaspoon finely grated orange peel

3 to 4 tablespoons orange juice

Soak the poppy seeds in the milk in a bowl for 2 hours. Mix the flour, baking powder and salt in a medium bowl.

Cream the butter in a mixer bowl until light. Add the sugar gradually, beating until fluffy. Beat in the eggs 1 at a time. Add 1 tablespoon orange peel, poppy seed mixture and vanilla and mix well.

Add the flour mixture alternately with 3/4 cup orange juice, beginning and ending with the flour and adding 1/4 cup orange juice at a time; mix well after each addition.

Spoon into a greased and floured 12-cup bundt pan. Bake at 350 degrees for 40 to 45 minutes or until a wooden pick inserted near the center comes out clean.

Cool in the pan on a wire rack for 15 minutes. Invert onto the wire rack to cool completely. Place a sheet of waxed paper under the rack.

Mix the confectioners' sugar and 1 teaspoon orange peel in a small bowl. Whisk in 3 to 4 tablespoons orange juice or enough to make of glazing consistency. Drizzle over the cake, allowing the glaze to drip down the side.

You may wrap in foil and store at room temperature for up to 3 days.

❧ YIELDS 16 SERVINGS

Black Walnut Pound Cake

1 cup butter, softened

1/2 cup shortening

3 cups sugar

5 eggs

3 cups flour

1 teaspoon baking powder

1 cup milk

1 teaspoon vanilla extract

1/2 teaspoon black walnut or
    almond extract

1 cup chopped black walnuts

Cream Cheese Frosting

Cream the butter, shortening and sugar in a large mixer bowl until light and fluffy. Beat in the eggs 1 at a time.

Sift the flour and baking powder together. Add to the creamed mixture alternately with the milk and flavorings, beating at low speed just until mixed. Fold in the walnuts.

Spoon into a greased and floured 10-inch tube pan. Bake at 325 degrees for 1 hour and 25 minutes or until the cake tests done.

Cool in the pan on a wire rack for 10 minutes. Remove to the wire rack to cool completely.

Frost with Cream Cheese Frosting.

❧ YIELDS 16 SERVINGS

Cream Cheese Frosting

8 ounces cream cheese,
    softened

1/4 cup butter, softened

1 (1-pound) package
    confectioners' sugar

1 teaspoon vanilla extract

Beat the cream cheese and butter in a mixer bowl until light.

Add the confectioners' sugar and vanilla and beat until fluffy.

❧ FROSTS 1 CAKE

Coconut Sour Cream Pound Cake

1½ cups butter, softened

3 cups sugar

6 eggs

3 cups flour

¼ teaspoon baking soda

¼ teaspoon salt

1 cup sour cream

1 (5- to 6-ounce) package frozen shredded coconut, thawed

1 teaspoon vanilla extract

Cream the butter and sugar in a mixer bowl until light and fluffy. Beat in the eggs 1 at a time.

Sift the flour, baking soda and salt together. Add to the creamed mixture alternately with the sour cream, mixing well after each addition. Beat in the coconut and vanilla.

Spoon into a greased and floured tube pan. Bake at 300 degrees for 1 hour to 1 hour and 20 minutes or until the cake tests done.

Cool in the pan for several minutes. Remove to a wire rack to cool completely.

❧ YIELDS 16 SERVINGS

Queen Anne's Lace

Queen Anne's Lace, a member of the carrot family, is a source of orange dye, a coffee substitute and a syrup. To add color to the lacey flowers, place a tablespoon of powdered, colored chalk in a bag. Insert flower heads, close the bag around the stems, and shake gently until flower heads are coated with the chalk. These make a beautiful centerpiece.

Light Pound Cake

1 cup butter, softened

1/2 cup shortening

3 cups sugar

5 eggs, beaten

3 cups sifted flour

1 teaspoon baking powder

1 teaspoon salt

1 cup milk

2 teaspoons vanilla or almond extract

Cream the butter and shortening in a mixer bowl until light. Add the sugar gradually, beating until fluffy. Beat in the eggs 1 at a time.

Mix the flour, baking powder and salt together. Add to the creamed mixture 1 spoonful at a time, alternating with the milk and mixing well after each addition. Add the vanilla and beat for 10 minutes.

Spoon into a greased bundt pan. Bake at 300 degrees for 1 1/2 hours.

Invert onto a pastry cloth and cover lightly with foil. Freeze for 8 hours or longer.

❧ YIELDS 16 SERVINGS

Wild Strawberry

This tasty fruit is rich in iron and potassium. Fresh strawberries remove tartar and stains from the teeth and can also lighten freckles. The strawberry leaf makes a calming herbal tea and is a toner for oily skin.

Pumpkin Roll

3 eggs

1 cup sugar

2/3 cup canned pumpkin

1 teaspoon lemon juice

3/4 cup flour

1 teaspoon baking powder

2 teaspoons cinnamon

1/2 teaspoon nutmeg

1/2 teaspoon salt

chopped nuts

1/4 cup confectioners' sugar

8 ounces cream cheese, softened

1/4 cup margarine, softened

1 1/2 cups confectioners' sugar

1/2 teaspoon vanilla extract

Beat the eggs at high speed in a mixer bowl for 3 minutes. Add the sugar gradually, beating constantly. Fold in the pumpkin and lemon juice.

Mix the flour, baking powder, cinnamon, nutmeg and salt together. Add to the pumpkin mixture and mix well.

Spoon into a greased and floured 9x13-inch cake pan. Sprinkle with chopped nuts. Bake at 375 degrees for 15 minutes. Cool in the pan for 5 minutes.

Invert onto a clean towel sprinkled with 1/4 cup confectioners' sugar. Roll up the cake in the towel. Let stand at room temperature for 3 hours or in the refrigerator for 15 minutes.

Beat the cream cheese and margarine with 1 1/2 cups confectioners' sugar and vanilla in a bowl until smooth.

Unroll the cake and spread with the confectioners' sugar filling. Roll the cake again to enclose the filling.

Garnish with additional confectioners' sugar.

❧ YIELDS 10 SERVINGS

Texas Sheet Cake

2 cups sugar

2 cups sifted flour

1 teaspoon baking soda

1/2 cup sour cream

2 eggs

1 teaspoon vanilla extract

1 cup butter or margarine

1 cup water

1/4 cup baking cocoa

Sheet Cake Frosting

Combine the sugar, flour, baking soda, sour cream, eggs and vanilla in a large mixer bowl and beat until smooth.

Combine the butter, water and cocoa in a saucepan. Bring to a boil. Add to the batter and mix until smooth.

Spoon into a greased and floured 10x15-inch cake pan. Bake at 350 degrees for 15 minutes or until a wooden pick inserted in the center comes out clean.

Frost immediately with the hot Sheet Cake Frosting.

❧ YIELDS 20 SERVINGS

Sheet Cake Frosting

1/2 cup butter or margarine

1/4 cup baking cocoa

6 tablespoons milk

1 (1-pound) package confectioners' sugar, sifted

1 cup chopped nuts

1 teaspoon vanilla extract

Melt the butter in a saucepan. Add the baking cocoa and milk. Bring to a boil and remove from the heat.

Add the confectioners' sugar, nuts and vanilla and mix well.

❧ FROSTS 1 SHEET CAKE

Swedish Butter Cake

6 eggs

2 cups sugar

2 cups cake flour

1 cup butter

Beat the eggs in a mixer bowl until foamy. Add the sugar gradually, beating constantly. Fold in the flour with a spatula.

Melt the butter in a small saucepan. Fold the hot butter into the batter.

Spoon into a greased bundt pan. Sprinkle with additional sugar.

Bake at 325 degrees for 45 to 60 minutes or until a tester inserted in the cake comes out clean. Cool in the pan for several minutes. Remove to a wire rack to cool completely.

You may substitute margarine for half of the butter in this recipe.

❧ YIELDS 16 SERVINGS

Mint

Peppermint, spearmint and pineapple mint are some of the distinctive, refreshing varieties of this perennial. Peppermint should be used sparingly in teas or cold drinks, while spearmint can enhance lamb, jellies, salads and chocolate. Pineapple mint provides an attractive garnish and adds zest to fruit salads or creamed cheeses.

Almond Ginger Wafers

1½ cups confectioners' sugar

1¼ cups flour

½ cup unsalted butter, chilled, sliced

1 tablespoon minced peeled fresh ginger

1 tablespoon ground ginger

½ teaspoon cinnamon

½ teaspoon salt

¾ cup toasted slivered almonds

3 tablespoons whipping cream

3 tablespoons chopped crystallized ginger

Combine the confectioners' sugar, flour, butter, fresh ginger, ground ginger, cinnamon and salt in a food processor. Pulse until the mixture resembles coarse crumbs.

Add the almonds, cream and crystallized ginger. Process just until moist clumps form.

Shape into 1¼-inch balls. Place on cookie sheets lined with baking parchment.

Moisten the bottom of a glass with water and dip into additional confectioners' sugar. Press the balls of dough to ¼-inch thickness.

Bake at 325 degrees for 28 minutes or until the cookies are golden brown on the bottoms and edges.

Remove to a wire rack to cool. Store in an airtight container at room temperature.

↜ YIELDS 2½ DOZEN

Ginger

Ground dried ginger is used for desserts and in savory dishes such as soups, meats, and curries. Its flavor is very different from the fresh form and cannot be substituted in dishes that use fresh ginger.

Apricot Biscotti

2 cups flour

1 teaspoon baking powder

¼ teaspoon baking soda

¼ teaspoon salt

¾ cup chopped pecans

¼ cup chopped dried apricots

2 eggs

½ cup sugar

½ cup vegetable oil

¼ cup flour

Mix 2 cups flour, baking powder, baking soda and salt in a large bowl. Add the pecans and apricots.

Beat the eggs and sugar in a large mixer bowl until thick and pale yellow. Add the oil and mix well. Add to the apricot mixture and mix to form a dough.

Knead in ¼ cup flour on a work surface. Shape into two 2x12-inch rolls. Place on a lightly greased cookie sheet.

Bake at 350 degrees for 30 minutes or until light brown. Cool slightly. Reduce the oven temperature to 275 degrees.

Slice the rolls diagonally ½ inch thick with a serrated knife. Arrange cut side down on ungreased cookie sheets.

Bake for 30 minutes longer, turning after 15 minutes. Remove to wire racks to cool. Store in airtight containers.

❧ YIELDS 3 DOZEN

Carolina Allspice

Carolina allspice was first used by Native Americans and is sometimes used as a substitute for cinnamon. Its scented roots, leaves and wood are popular ingredients in potpourri.

Special Fudge Brownies

1/4 cup Sugar Twin

6 packets Equal

1/2 cup melted margarine

2 large eggs

1 teaspoon vanilla extract

1/3 cup flour

1/3 cup baking cocoa

Combine the Sugar Twin, Equal, margarine, eggs and vanilla in a medium bowl and mix well.

Mix the flour and baking cocoa together. Add to the egg mixture and mix well.

Spread in an 8x8-inch baking pan sprayed with nonstick cooking spray. Bake at 350 degrees for 25 minutes.

Cool on a wire rack. Cut into 2-inch squares. Add 1/2 cup chopped pecans if desired.

❧ YIELDS 1 1/4 DOZEN

Chiffon Nut Bars

2 eggs

1 cup packed brown sugar

1/2 cup vegetable oil

1 teaspoon vanilla extract

1/4 teaspoon salt

1/2 cup sifted flour

1 cup coarsely chopped nuts

Beat the eggs in a mixer bowl until thick and pale yellow. Add the brown sugar gradually, beating constantly until the brown sugar dissolves.

Stir in the oil, vanilla and salt. Fold in the flour and 3/4 cup of the nuts.

Spoon into a greased 7x11-inch baking pan; sprinkle with the remaining 1/4 cup nuts.

Bake at 350 degrees for 20 minutes or until a wooden pick inserted in the center comes out clean. Cool on a wire rack for 5 minutes.

Cut into bars while warm and remove from the pan.

❧ YIELDS 2 DOZEN

Chinese Chews

3/4 cup flour, sifted

1 cup sugar

1 teaspoon baking powder

1/4 teaspoon salt

3 eggs, beaten

1 cup broken walnuts

1 cup chopped dates

Sift the flour, sugar, baking powder and salt into a large bowl. Add the eggs, walnuts and dates and mix well.

Spoon into a greased and floured 10x15-inch baking pan. Bake at 350 degrees for 15 minutes or until golden brown. Cool on a wire rack for 5 minutes.

Cut into bars while warm and remove from the pan.

❧ YIELDS 3 DOZEN

Christmas Holly Cookies

1/3 cup butter

16 marshmallows

1 teaspoon vanilla extract

green food coloring

2 1/2 cups cornflakes

red cinnamon candies

Melt the butter in a double boiler. Add the marshmallows. Heat until the marshmallows melt, stirring to mix well; remove from the heat.

Stir in the vanilla and food coloring. Add the cornflakes and mix until coated.

Drop by tablespoonfuls onto waxed paper. Press 3 or 4 cinnamon candies onto each cookie to resemble berries. Let stand for 2 days or longer.

❧ YIELDS 3 DOZEN

Date Bars

1 cup chopped dates

1 cup sugar

1 cup water

1 cup chopped nuts (optional)

1³⁄₄ cups rolled oats

1¹⁄₂ cups flour

1 cup packed brown sugar

1 teaspoon baking soda

³⁄₄ cup butter

confectioners' sugar

Combine the dates with the sugar and water in a saucepan. Cook until the dates are mushy. Stir in the nuts.

Combine the oats, flour, brown sugar, baking soda and butter in a bowl and mix until crumbly.

Press half the crumb mixture over the bottom of a 9x12-inch baking dish. Spread the date mixture in the prepared dish and top with the remaining crumbs. Sprinkle with confectioners' sugar.

Bake at 350 degrees for 20 minutes. Cool on a wire rack. Cut into bars.

✎ YIELDS 2 DOZEN

Herb ABCs

Arrange herbs and spices in alphabetical order on your spice shelf to eliminate searching for the correct one.

Gingersnaps

3/4 cup margarine, softened

1 cup sugar

1 egg

2 cups flour

2 teaspoons baking soda

1 teaspoon ground cloves

1 teaspoon ground cinnamon

1 teaspoon ground ginger

1/4 teaspoon salt

1/4 cup molasses

Cream the margarine and sugar in a mixer bowl until light and fluffy. Beat in the egg.

Sift the flour, baking soda, cloves, cinnamon, ginger and salt together. Add to the creamed mixture with the molasses and mix well.

Drop by 1/2 teaspoonfuls onto a greased cookie sheet. Bake at 325 degrees for 8 to 10 minutes or until set; the cookies will become crisp as they cool.

Cool on the cookie sheet for several minutes. Remove to a wire rack to cool completely. Store in an airtight container.

❧ YIELDS 6 DOZEN

Buying Herbs and Spices

Buy herbs and spices in small amounts to retain their peak flavor. Date each as you buy it and replace it after one year for maximum flavor.

Mexican Wedding Cookies

1 cup butter or margarine, softened

½ cup confectioners' sugar

2 cups sifted cake flour

1 teaspoon vanilla extract

1 teaspoon almond extract

1 teaspoon walnut extract

2 cups chopped pecans

confectioners' sugar

Cream the butter and confectioners' sugar in a mixer bowl until light and fluffy.

Add the flour and flavorings and mix well. Mix in the pecans.

Shape into small balls and place on a greased cookie sheet.

Bake at 350 degrees for 15 minutes. Roll the warm cookies in confectioners' sugar. Cool on a wire rack.

❧ YIELDS 8 DOZEN

Pecan Balls

1 cup butter, softened

¼ cup sugar

2 cups cake flour

2 cups chopped pecans

2 teaspoons vanilla extract

confectioners' sugar

Cream the butter and sugar in a mixer bowl until light and fluffy. Add the flour, pecans and vanilla and mix well.

Shape into small balls and place on a greased cookie sheet.

Bake at 325 degrees for 25 minutes. Roll the warm cookies in confectioners' sugar. Cool on a wire rack. Roll the cooled cookies in confectioners' sugar.

You may need to mix this with your hands.

❧ YIELDS 8 DOZEN

Toffee Bars

1 cup margarine, softened

2 cups packed brown sugar

1 egg yolk

1 teaspoon vanilla extract

2 cups flour

1 (6-ounce) package semisweet chocolate chips

1 cup chopped walnuts or pecans

Beat the margarine in a mixer bowl for 30 seconds. Add the brown sugar gradually, beating until smooth.

Beat in the egg yolk and vanilla. Add the flour gradually, beating constantly. Stir in the chocolate chips and walnuts.

Press evenly over the bottom of an ungreased 10x15-inch baking pan. Bake at 350 degrees for 15 to 18 minutes or until set.

Cut into bars while warm. Cool on a wire rack and remove from the pan.

❧ YIELDS 4 DOZEN

Triple-A Bars

1 cup margarine, softened

1 cup packed light brown sugar

1 egg yolk

2 cups flour

1 tablespoon vanilla extract

8 ounces semisweet chocolate chips

3 ounces finely ground walnuts

Combine the margarine, brown sugar and egg yolk in a mixer bowl and beat until smooth.

Add the flour and vanilla. Press over the bottom of a 10x15-inch baking pan.

Bake at 350 degrees for 15 to 20 minutes or until golden brown.

Melt the chocolate chips in a double boiler. Spread over the hot layer and sprinkle with the walnuts.

Cool on a wire rack. Cut into small bars.

❧ YIELDS 4 TO 5 DOZEN

Chocolate Pecan Turtle Bars

1 (2-layer) package devil's
food cake mix

1 (14-ounce) package caramel
candies

½ cup evaporated milk

½ cup butter

1 (6-ounce) package milk
chocolate chips

1 cup chopped pecans

Prepare the cake mix using the package directions.
Spread half the batter in a greased and floured 9x13-
inch baking pan.

Bake at 350 degrees for 15 minutes.

Unwrap the caramels and combine with the
evaporated milk and butter in a double boiler.
Melt over hot water, stirring to blend well.

Remove the baked layer from the oven and sprinkle
with the chocolate chips and pecans. Spread the
caramel mixture evenly over the baked layer. Spread
the remaining cake batter over the top.

Bake for 30 minutes longer. Cool on a wire rack.
Cut into 2-inch bars.

❧ YIELDS 2 DOZEN

Desserts
Pies
Candy

Volunteers Are . . .

*Volunteers are the only human
beings on the face of the earth who reflect
this nation's compassion, unselfish
caring, patience, and just plain
loving one another.*

ERMA BOMBECK

Amaretto Cheesecake

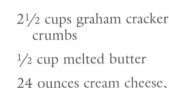

2½ cups graham cracker crumbs

½ cup melted butter

24 ounces cream cheese, softened

1 cup sugar

4 eggs

1 teaspoon vanilla extract

2 tablespoons amaretto

1 teaspoon almond extract

2 cups sour cream

¼ cup sugar

2 tablespoons amaretto

Mix the graham cracker crumbs and melted butter in a bowl. Press into an 8½-inch springform pan.

Combine the cream cheese, 1 cup sugar, eggs and vanilla in a mixer bowl and beat until smooth. Beat in 2 tablespoons amaretto and the almond extract.

Spoon evenly into the prepared pan. Bake at 325 degrees for 40 minutes until a wooden pick inserted in the center comes out clean. Cool for 10 minutes.

Mix the sour cream with ¼ cup sugar and 2 tablespoons amaretto in a small bowl. Spread over the cheesecake, swirling from the outer edge to the center.

Bake for 10 minutes longer. Cool on a wire rack for 4 to 5 hours. Chill for 8 hours or longer.

Place on a serving plate and remove the side of the pan.

❧ YIELDS 12 SERVINGS

Apple Dumplings

1 (10-count) can butter-style
  biscuits

6 cooking apples, peeled,
  finely chopped

cinnamon to taste

5 teaspoons butter

3 cups water

2 cups sugar

½ cup margarine

Roll the biscuits very thin on a floured surface.

Place ½ cup apple on each biscuit. Sprinkle with cinnamon and dot with butter.

Pull up the edges of the biscuits to enclose the apples and press firmly to seal. Arrange in a 9x13-inch baking pan.

Bring the water, sugar and margarine to a boil in a saucepan. Pour around the dumplings in the pan.

Bake at 375 degrees for 35 to 45 minutes or until golden brown. Serve warm.

❧ YIELDS 10 SERVINGS

Pansy

Similar in taste to Johnny-jump-ups, pansies are often used to garnish desserts or to float in cold drinks or soups. The flowers of this very hardy annual come in every color of the rainbow and should be picked when they first open.

From-Scratch Banana Pudding

1 package vanilla wafers

8 bananas, sliced

2 tablespoons cornstarch

2 cups milk

2 egg yolks

1/2 cup sugar

1 tablespoon vanilla extract

2 egg whites

1 tablespoon cold water

1 teaspoon vanilla extract

1/4 cup sugar

Alternate layers of vanilla wafers and banana slices to the top of a 5x9-inch loaf pan.

Blend the cornstarch with a small amount of the milk in a double boiler. Add the remaining milk, egg yolks, 1/2 cup sugar and 1 tablespoon vanilla and mix well. Cook over hot water until thickened, stirring constantly.

Pour over the layers in the loaf pan. Cut through the mixture with a knife 3 times lengthwise and 5 times crosswise to allow the pudding mixture to penetrate.

Combine the egg whites with the cold water in a mixer bowl. Beat for 1 minute. Add 1 teaspoon vanilla and 1/4 cup sugar and beat until stiff peaks form. Spread over the pudding, sealing to the edge of the pan.

Bake at 350 degrees just until the meringue is golden brown.

❧ YIELDS 6 SERVINGS

Substitution

As a general rule, you can substitute three to four times the amount of fresh herbs for dried herbs.

Boiled Custard

1 quart milk

1 cup sugar

4 egg yolks, beaten

1 teaspoon (or more) vanilla
    extract

Heat the milk and sugar in a saucepan just until it is hot to the finger.

Stir 1 cup of the hot milk mixture into the beaten egg yolks; stir the egg yolks gradually into the hot milk.

Cook over medium heat until the mixture coats a spoon, stirring occasionally; remove from the heat. Cool slightly, stirring occasionally. Stir in the vanilla.

Serve warm or chilled in a glass or over meringues with ice cream or fruit.

❧ YIELDS 8 SERVINGS

Chocolate Fudge Sauce

1½ tablespoons flour

1 cup sugar

2½ tablespoons baking cocoa

1 cup evaporated milk

1 teaspoon vanilla extract

1 tablespoon butter or
    margarine

Mix the flour, sugar and baking cocoa in a heavy saucepan. Add the evaporated milk gradually, stirring to mix well.

Cook over low heat until thickened and smooth, stirring constantly; remove from the heat. Stir in the vanilla and butter.

Serve hot or cold over cake and/or ice cream. The sauce may be reheated in the microwave.

❧ YIELDS 1½ CUPS

Coffee Charlotte Russe

2 envelopes unflavored gelatin

1/2 cup sugar

1/4 cup (scant) instant coffee powder

1/4 teaspoon salt

4 egg yolks

2 1/2 cups milk

1 teaspoon vanilla extract

3 1/2 to 4 dozen ladyfingers

4 egg whites

1/2 cup sugar

2 cups whipping cream, whipped

Mix the gelatin, 1/2 cup sugar, coffee powder and salt in a double boiler. Beat the egg yolks with the milk in a small bowl. Add to the coffee mixture. Let stand for 1 minute.

Cook over boiling water for 10 minutes or until the gelatin dissolves completely, stirring constantly; remove from the heat. Stir in the vanilla.

Chill for several hours or until the mixture mounds slightly when dropped from a spoon, stirring occasionally.

Line the bottom and side of a 10-inch springform pan with ladyfingers.

Beat the egg whites until foamy. Add 1/2 cup sugar gradually, beating until stiff peaks form. Fold in the gelatin mixture. Fold in the whipped cream.

Spoon into the springform pan. Chill until firm. Place on a serving plate; remove the side of the pan.

Garnish with additional whipped cream, pecans or grated or shaved chocolate.

You may dip the tips of the ladyfingers into a mixture of melted semisweet chocolate, sugar and butter.

❧ YIELDS 12 TO 14 SERVINGS

Dutch Brick Dessert

8 (1-ounce) squares
   semisweet chocolate

8 ounces shortening

3 eggs, beaten

3 tablespoons sugar

1 tablespoon rum

2 packages shortbread cookies

Melt the chocolate with the shortening in a double boiler over hot water.

Add the eggs very gradually, stirring constantly. Stir in the sugar and rum; remove from the heat.

Arrange a layer of cookies in a greased 5x9-inch loaf pan. Spread ¼ inch of the chocolate mixture over the cookies.

Repeat the layers until all the ingredients are used.

Chill for 8 hours or longer. Cut into ½-inch slices and serve with whipped cream.

❧ YIELDS 15 SERVINGS

Daisy

A perennial flower which has a mild flavor, the daisy can be eaten fresh in salads or be used as a garnish. Blooming from April to September, the petals can be white or pink in color surrounding a yellow center. Plant six inches apart in full sun.

Lemon-Pecan Dessert

1 (2-layer) package lemon
   supreme cake mix

½ cup margarine, softened

1 egg

1 teaspoon vanilla extract

salt to taste

1 cup chopped pecans

8 ounces cream cheese,
   softened

2 eggs

1 (1-pound) package
   confectioners' sugar

Combine the cake mix, margarine, 1 egg, vanilla and salt in a bowl. Knead or mix to form a dough.

Press the dough evenly into a lightly greased 9x13-inch baking pan. Sprinkle with the pecans.

Beat the cream cheese in a mixer bowl until light. Beat in 2 eggs 1 at a time. Add the confectioners' sugar and beat until smooth. Spread over the pecans.

Bake at 350 degrees for 35 minutes; do not undercook. Cool on a wire rack. Cut into squares.

❧ YIELDS 15 SERVINGS

Herb Seasoning

Reduce sodium intake by seasoning with herbs. Make an all-purpose seasoning of two teaspoons each of marjoram, coriander and paprika, one-half teaspoon of dry mustard and one-eighth teaspoon of garlic powder.

Next Best Thing to Robert Redford

1 cup flour

½ cup butter

1 cup chopped nuts

8 ounces cream cheese, softened

1 cup sugar

8 ounces whipped topping

1 (4-ounce) package vanilla instant pudding mix

1 (4-ounce) package chocolate instant pudding mix

3 cups milk

Mix the flour, butter and nuts in a bowl. Press into a 9x13-inch baking dish.

Bake at 350 degrees for 20 minutes or until brown. Cool to room temperature.

Beat the cream cheese with the sugar in a mixer bowl until light and fluffy. Fold in half the whipped topping. Spread over the cooled layer.

Combine the pudding mixes with the milk in a mixer bowl. Beat until thickened and smooth. Spread over the cream cheese layer. Spread the remaining whipped topping over the pudding layer.

Garnish with grated chocolate. Chill, covered, until serving time.

❧ YIELDS 12 SERVINGS

Wax Myrtle

Berries from the wax myrtle yield balsamic scented wax used in candles, shaving cream, and cosmetics. Tonics made from the roots are astringent and antibacterial.

Old-Fashioned Apple Pie

1 recipe (2-crust) pie pastry

1 cup sugar

2 teaspoons flour

1/4 teaspoon nutmeg

1/2 teaspoon cinnamon

6 to 8 large tart apples, peeled, thinly sliced

2 tablespoons butter or margarine

Roll half the pastry on a floured surface and place in a 9-inch pie plate.

Mix the sugar, flour, nutmeg and cinnamon in a bowl. Sprinkle a small amount of the flour mixture over the pastry in the pie plate.

Arrange the apples in the prepared pan and sprinkle with the remaining flour mixture. Dot with the butter.

Roll the remaining pastry on a floured surface and place over the pie filling. Trim and seal the pastry, fluting the edge. Cut vents in the top.

Bake at 400 degrees for 50 to 60 minutes or until the crust is golden brown.

❧ YIELDS 6 TO 8 SERVINGS

Johnny-Jump-Up

Blooming with brilliant violet, white, purple or yellow flowers—or a combination of all four—this is thought to be a parent of the pansy. Johnny-jump-up flowers make a pretty candied garnish on a dessert or can brighten up a spring salad or punch bowl. Its mild taste is reminiscent of sweet baby lettuce.

Apple Pie with Crumb Crust

6½ cups sliced peeled apples, about 13 to 15 apples

1 tablespoon lemon juice

¾ cup sugar

⅓ cup packed brown sugar

2 to 2½ tablespoons minute tapioca

1½ teaspoons apple pie spice

¼ teaspoon salt

3 to 4 tablespoons melted butter or sliced butter

½ cup flour

½ cup packed brown sugar

¼ cup butter

½ cup walnuts

Combine the apples with the lemon juice, sugar, ⅓ cup brown sugar, tapioca, apple pie spice and salt in a bowl; toss to mix well.

Spoon into a 10-inch deep-dish pie plate. Drizzle with the melted butter.

Combine the flour, ½ cup brown sugar, ¼ cup butter and walnuts in a bowl. Mix with a pastry blender until crumbly. Press over the apple filling.

Bake at 350 degrees for 1 hour.

This can also be prepared in 2 unbaked pie shells.

❧ YIELDS 10 TO 12 SERVINGS

Nutmeg

Nutmeg, the seed of a tropical evergreen, is sold whole or ground. It has a flavor and aroma that are delicately warm, spicy and sweet. This spice is especially good in baked goods, custards, and fruit dishes.

Buttermilk Pie

2¼ cups sugar

½ cup flour

2 cups buttermilk

2 eggs, beaten

½ cup melted butter

1 tablespoon lemon extract

2 unbaked pie shells

Mix the sugar and flour in a bowl. Blend in a small amount of the buttermilk.

Add the remaining buttermilk, eggs, melted butter and lemon extract; mix well. Spoon into the pie shells.

Bake at 325 degrees for 1 hour or until golden brown.

❧ YIELDS 2 PIES

Cherry Cheese Pie

1 (21-ounce) can cherry pie filling

1 tablespoon lemon juice

¼ cup sugar

1 unbaked (9-inch) pie shell

8 ounces cream cheese, softened

½ cup sugar

2 eggs

1 teaspoon vanilla extract

nutmeg

Combine the cherry pie filling, lemon juice and ¼ cup sugar in a bowl and mix well. Spoon into the pie shell.

Bake at 425 degrees for 15 minutes; reduce the oven temperature to 350 degrees.

Combine the cream cheese, ½ cup sugar, eggs and vanilla in a mixer bowl and beat until smooth. Spread over the cherry mixture. Sprinkle with nutmeg.

Bake for 30 minutes longer or until the topping is set.

❧ YIELDS 6 TO 8 SERVINGS

German Chocolate Pie

1 cup sugar

2 tablespoons flour

1 tablespoon cornstarch

2 tablespoons baking cocoa

salt to taste

2 eggs, slightly beaten

3 tablespoons melted
   margarine

2/3 cup milk

1 teaspoon vanilla extract

3/4 cup shredded coconut

1/3 cup chopped pecans

1 unbaked pie shell

Mix the sugar, flour, cornstarch, baking cocoa and salt in a bowl.

Add the eggs, margarine, milk and vanilla and mix until smooth.

Stir in the coconut and pecans. Spoon into the pie shell.

Bake at 400 degrees for 30 minutes.

❧ YIELDS 6 TO 8 SERVINGS

Anise Hyssop

Used in soups, baked goods, tea and sugar and
complementary with cinnamon and bay leaves, anise
hyssop is a perennial herb. Native Americans used the
licorice-tasting leaves as a sweetener and the roots
as a cough remedy. This self-sowing plant blooms
with dusky indigo spikes in July.

Chocolate Pecan Pie

2 (1-ounce) squares
   unsweetened chocolate

3 tablespoons butter

1 cup light corn syrup

¾ cup sugar

3 eggs, slightly beaten

1 teaspoon vanilla extract

1 cup coarsely chopped
   pecans

1 unbaked (9-inch) pie shell

Melt the chocolate with the butter in a double boiler over boiling water.

Combine the corn syrup and sugar in a small saucepan. Bring to a boil and boil for 2 minutes. Add the chocolate mixture and mix well.

Stir a small amount of the hot mixture into the eggs; stir the eggs into the hot mixture. Add the vanilla and pecans.

Spoon into the pie shell. Bake at 350 degrees for 45 to 60 minutes or until the pie is puffed and set. Cool completely.

Serve with whipped cream or ice cream.

❧ YIELDS 8 SERVINGS

Vanilla

Vanilla is made from the bean of the only orchid
that bears edible fruit. It is used in many dishes,
but especially heightens the flavor of chocolate.

Impossible Coconut Pie

1¾ cups sugar

½ cup self-rising flour

4 eggs

2 cups milk

¼ cup melted butter

1 teaspoon vanilla extract

7 ounces shredded coconut

Mix the sugar and flour in a bowl. Add the eggs, milk, butter and vanilla and mix well. Stir in the coconut.

Spoon into 2 greased 9-inch pie plates. Bake at 350 degrees for 30 minutes or until golden brown.

You may add pecans or berries to this recipe.

❧ YIELDS 2 PIES

Meringue Pie

3 egg whites

1 cup sugar

1 teaspoon almond extract

12 crackers, finely crushed

12 dates, finely chopped

½ cup coarsely chopped almonds, walnuts or pecans

Beat the egg whites in a mixer bowl until stiff but not dry peaks form.

Fold in the sugar and almond extract. Fold in the cracker crumbs, dates and almonds.

Spoon into a buttered 8- or 9-inch pie plate.

Bake at 350 degrees for 30 minutes.

Serve with whipped topping or chocolate ice cream.

❧ YIELDS 6 TO 8 SERVINGS

Million-Dollar Pie

16 ounces whipped topping

1 (14-ounce) can sweetened condensed milk

1 (15-ounce) can crushed pineapple, drained

1 (6-ounce) jar maraschino cherries, drained, chopped

1½ cups chopped pecans

2½ tablespoons fresh lemon juice

2 (9-inch) graham cracker pie shells

Combine the whipped topping and condensed milk in a bowl and mix well.

Stir in the pineapple, cherries and pecans. Add the lemon juice and mix until thickened.

Spoon into the pie shells. Chill until serving time.

❧ YIELDS 2 PIES

Scented Geraniums

A perennial generally grown as an annual or a houseplant, geraniums come in a wide variety of colors (white, purple, yellow) and scents (lemon, nutmeg, ginger, peppermint, rose), which are released by being rubbed or by the hot sun. It is used in baked goods, ice creams, jellies, candied garnishes and scented sugar.

Bourbon Peach Pie

1¼ cups whole wheat flour

¾ cup all-purpose flour

¾ teaspoon salt

¾ cup unsalted butter, chilled, sliced

7 tablespoons cold water

2½ pounds fresh peaches

½ cup sugar

½ cup packed light brown sugar

4 teaspoons quick-cooking tapioca

2 to 3 teaspoons bourbon

½ teaspoon ground cardamom

1 teaspoon grated lemon peel

Combine the whole wheat flour, all-purpose flour, salt and butter in a food processor and process for 40 seconds or until of the consistency of coarse meal.

Add the cold water. Process just until the mixture begins to form a ball.

Divide into 2 portions, 1 slightly larger than the other. Wrap each in plastic wrap and chill for 1 hour or until firm.

Blanch the peaches in boiling water in a saucepan for 30 seconds; drain and cool slightly. Peel and cut into wedges; the peaches should measure about 6 cups.

Combine the peaches with the sugar, brown sugar, tapioca, bourbon, cardamom and lemon peel in a bowl and stir to mix well. Let stand for 15 minutes.

Roll the larger portion of pastry to a 14-inch circle on a floured surface. Fit into a 9-inch plate. Spoon the peach filling into the prepared pie plate.

Roll the remaining pastry and place over the peaches. Seal the pastry and crimp into a decorative stand-up edge. Cut vents in the top.

Place on a foil-covered baking sheet and tent with foil. Bake at 375 degrees for 1 hour. Remove the foil tent. Bake for 15 minutes longer or until the filling is bubbly and the crust is golden brown. Cool to room temperature.

❧ YIELDS 8 SERVINGS

Pecan Pie

1¼ cups packed brown sugar

2 tablespoons cornstarch

1 cup light corn syrup

6 eggs

½ cup melted butter

1 teaspoon vanilla extract

1 cup chopped pecans

1 unbaked pie shell

Mix the brown sugar and cornstarch in a bowl. Add the corn syrup, eggs, butter and vanilla and mix well. Stir in the pecans.

Spoon into the pie shell. Bake at 325 degrees for 45 minutes or until the crust is golden brown and the filling is set.

❧ YIELDS 6 TO 8 SERVINGS

Company Pecan Pie

2 unbaked (8- or 9-inch) pie shells

½ cup melted butter

½ cup sugar

¾ cup light corn syrup

¼ cup dark corn syrup

1 tablespoon vanilla extract

2 cups pecans

3 eggs, beaten

Bake the pie shells at 225 degrees just until they appear dry. Remove from the oven and increase the oven temperature to 325 degrees.

Combine the butter, sugar, corn syrups and vanilla in a bowl and mix well. Stir in the pecans. Fold in the eggs.

Spoon into the pie shells. Bake for 1 hour.

❧ YIELDS 2 PIES

Pineapple Chiffon Pie

4 egg yolks

¼ cup sugar

¼ teaspoon salt

1 cup water

1 (3-ounce) package lemon
gelatin

1 cup crushed pineapple with
juice

4 egg whites

¼ cup sugar

1 baked (10-inch) pie shell

Combine the egg yolks, ¼ cup sugar and salt in a mixer bowl and beat until thick and pale yellow.

Bring the water to a boil in a saucepan. Add the gelatin and stir until completely dissolved. Add very gradually to the egg yolk mixture, beating constantly. Stir in the undrained pineapple.

Chill just until the mixture begins to thicken. Beat just until smooth.

Beat the egg whites until foamy. Add ¼ cup sugar gradually, beating until stiff peaks form. Fold into the gelatin mixture.

Spoon into the pie shell. Chill until serving time.

Garnish servings with sweetened whipped cream.

❧ YIELDS 8 SERVINGS

Clove Pink

The wild ancestor of the modern carnation, clove pink
has a spicy, mild clove flavor. The semi-double fragrant
flowers of this perennial are pink to rose-purple
in color and can be used fresh to flavor syrups, fruit
cups or beverages, but be sure to remove the
bitter white base first.

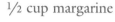

Pineapple Coconut Pie

½ cup margarine

2 cups sugar

4 eggs, slightly beaten

1 (8-ounce) can crushed
  pineapple

1 cup shredded coconut

2 unbaked pie shells

Melt the margarine in a saucepan. Combine with the sugar and eggs in a bowl and mix well.

Stir in the undrained pineapple and coconut.

Spoon into the pie shells. Bake at 325 degrees for 40 minutes or until golden brown.

❧ YIELDS 2 PIES

Pumpkin and Bourbon Pie for Diabetics

1 (15-ounce) can pumpkin

2 eggs

1 cup evaporated milk

½ cup bourbon

2 tablespoons NutraSweet

1 tablespoon Brown Sugar
  Twin

4 to 5 packets NutraTaste

1 teaspoon ground cinnamon

½ teaspoon ground ginger

¼ teaspoon ground cloves

½ teaspoon salt

1 teaspoon vanilla extract

1 unbaked (9-inch) deep-dish
  pie shell

Combine the pumpkin, eggs, evaporated milk and bourbon in a blender.

Add the sweeteners, cinnamon, ginger, cloves, salt and vanilla. Process until smooth.

Spoon into the pie shell. Bake at 350 degrees for 1 hour or until a knife inserted in the center comes out clean.

You may substitute additional evaporated milk for all or part of the bourbon. You may vary the spices to taste.

❧ YIELDS 8 SERVINGS

Sweet Potato Pie

3 or 4 sweet potatoes, boiled or baked, peeled

½ cup butter, softened

2 cups sugar

4 eggs

1 (12-ounce) can evaporated milk

1 teaspoon cinnamon

½ teaspoon nutmeg

¼ teaspoon ground cloves

½ teaspoon salt

2 unbaked (9-inch) deep-dish pie shells

Beat the sweet potatoes in a mixer bowl until smooth. Add the butter and sugar and mix well. Beat in the eggs 1 at a time.

Add the evaporated milk, cinnamon, nutmeg, cloves and salt and mix well.

Spoon into the pie shells. Bake at 375 degrees for 1 hour and 10 minutes or until a knife inserted in the center comes out clean. Cool on wire racks.

Garnish with marshmallows.

🐦 YIELDS 2 PIES

Decorative Herbs

Tarragon, thyme, savory and sage make a very attractive combination of herbs to grow in a large hanging basket. It will be both pretty to look at and easy to use.

Never-Fail Fudge

5 cups sugar

1 cup evaporated milk

¾ cup margarine

1 (13-ounce) jar marshmallow
  creme

3 cups chocolate chips

2 cups chopped pecans

Combine the sugar, evaporated milk and margarine in a heavy saucepan. Bring to a boil. Cook for 8 to 10 minutes.

Combine the marshmallow creme, chocolate chips and pecans in a large bowl. Add the hot mixture and mix quickly.

Spoon immediately into a greased 10x15-inch pan. Let stand until cool. Cut into squares.

☙ YIELDS 7 DOZEN SMALL SQUARES

Tulip

Like the nasturtium, these brightly-colored flowers
are best used as a garnish or a container of a cold dish,
such as chicken or egg salad. Tulips bloom in mid to
late spring and their light flavor is similar in taste to
peas. The best variety for culinary use is the Darwin
hybrid, which has a large, single flower.

Chocolate Crunchies

1 sleeve crackers

1 cup packed brown sugar

1 cup butter

1 (12-ounce) package
   chocolate chips

Arrange the crackers on a foil-lined 10x15-inch baking pan.

Bring the brown sugar and butter to a boil in a saucepan. Boil for 3 minutes, stirring constantly. Spoon over the crackers.

Bake at 400 degrees for 7 minutes, checking occasionally to prevent overbrowning; remove from the oven.

Sprinkle with the chocolate chips. Let stand until the chocolate chips begin to melt and spread evenly over the top. Cool in the refrigerator or freezer. Break into pieces. Store in the refrigerator or freezer.

Do not substitute margarine for the butter in this recipe.

✎ YIELDS 20 SERVINGS

Peanut Butter Balls

2 cups peanut butter

3/4 cup margarine, softened

1 (1-pound) package
   confectioners' sugar

1 pound milk chocolate chips

1 square paraffin

Combine the peanut butter, margarine and confectioners' sugar in a bowl; mix until smooth. Shape into balls.

Melt the chocolate chips with the paraffin in a double boiler. Dip the balls into the melted chocolate, coating well.

Place on waxed paper and let stand until the chocolate is set.

✎ YIELDS 3 1/2 POUNDS

Contributors List

Betty Ames
Betty Andrews
Alice Arledge
Margaret Armield
Carrie Artis
Allison Atkinson
Carter Baynes
Margurite Bellios
Shirley Benson
Cynthia Benton
Dorothy Bishop
Caroline Bock
Augusta B. Bordeaux
Barbara Brodbeck
Sylvia Brown
Peggy Bryan
Annie 'Pearl' Bunn
Elizabeth Burney
Avis Calabro
Bea Carlson
Joanne Carson
Betty Lou Collins
Rushie Wrenn Collins
Ann B. Compton
Sherry Davis
Alice Demcio
Earline Edwards
Patricia Ferguson
Janet Fisch
Jim Fisch

Katherine Furr
Sarah Godwin
Nancy Gray
Daisy Hassin
Lynn Hatch
Carol Hosmer
Doris Hughs
Gertrude Hunter
Burnette Jones
Dick Jones
Nancy Jones
Frances Jordon
Anne Kane
Kath Keenan
Audrey Klumpennar
Audrey Lamb
Doris Manzo
Margaret Martin
Joyce Matthis
Betty Matzke
Virginia Moore
Linda Mueller
Jann Nance
Shirley Nolan
Fran Page
Ruth Paxton
Louise Perkins
Emma Powell
Sue Powell
Rachel Pridgen

Stephen A. Purvis
Helen Quinn
Marian Rippy
Wilhelmenia Rogers
Lil Romanek
Dennis Rushing
Sherry Sansone
Lillie Belle Scott
Louis Shrier
John Simon
Dixey A. Smith
Anna Snyder
Sarah Sowers
Peggye J. Stanley
Buddy Stapins
Bea Stewart
Betty Stines
Joni Sturdy
Exalene Sullivan
Margie Sullivan
Harriette Taylor
Bebe Thompson
Tonda Verdejo
Libby Waldkirch
Millie Warlick
Betsy Watkins
Mary Weingert
Bob White
Fran Williams

Index

Accompaniments
Apple and Cranberry
Relish, 101
Barbecue Sauce, 59
Freezer Pickles, 102
Magnolia's Blackening
Spice, 58

Appetizers
Black-Eyed Peas con
Queso, 12
Guacamole Dip, 12
Ham Rolls, 8
Hot Artichoke Dip, 11
Hot Cheese and Crab
Dip, 11
Layered Taco Dip, 14
Mexican Roll-Ups, 8
Mozzarella Cheese
Puffs, 9
Pickled Shrimp, 10
Pineapple Cheese
Ball, 16
Pizza Rounds, 9
Rosedale Dip, 15
Shrimp Mold, 17
Shrimp Spread, 18
South-of-the-Border
Dip, 13
Spinach Dip, 15
Strawberry Cheese
Ring, 16
Vegetable Spread, 19

Apple
Apple and Cranberry
Casserole, 100
Apple and Cranberry
Relish, 101
Apple and Raisin
Cake, 104
Apple Cake, 105
Apple Dumplings, 133
Apple Pie with Crumb
Crust, 141

Old-Fashioned Apple
Pie, 140

Apricot
Apricot and Orange
Salad, 27
Apricot Biscotti, 123
Apricot Chicken, 64

Asparagus
Asparagus Casserole, 82
Asparagus Swiss
Soufflé, 83
Cheddar Cheese and
Asparagus Soup, 22

Beans
Barbecued Beans, 84
Calico Beans, 85
Different Potato and
Bean Casserole, 90
Green Bean and Corn
Casserole, 86
Marinated Bean
Salad, 33

Beef
Baked Spaghetti, 53
Beef and Vegetable
Soup, 23
California Casserole, 50
Chili, 51
Chinese Spaghetti, 54
Easy Swiss Steak, 48
Golfers' Stew, 55
Lobster-Stuffed Beef
Tenderloin, 49
Pizza Rounds, 9
Porcupines, 52
Prize-Winning Meat
Loaf, 52
Red Flannel Hash, 51
Santa Fe Stew, 56
Saucy Sirloin
Surprise, 48

Beverages
Champagne Punch, 20
White Sangria, 20

Blueberry
Blueberry Bread, 42
Blueberry Muffins, 43

Breads
Banana Nut Bread, 41
Blueberry Bread, 42
Blueberry Muffins, 43
Broccoli Corn
Bread, 39
Cornmeal Muffins, 40
Corny Corn Bread, 40
Irish Soda Bread, 46
Lemon Nut Bread, 44
Norwegian Bread, 45
Nut Bread, 43

Broccoli
Broccoli and Corn
Casserole, 87
Broccoli Casserole, 87
Broccoli Corn
Bread, 39
Broccoli with
Noodles, 88
Sesame Broccoli, 88

Cabbage
Asian Coleslaw, 36
Old South Cabbage
Slaw, 35

Cakes
Apple and Raisin
Cake, 104
Apple Cake, 105
Black Walnut Pound
Cake, 116
Blackberry Wine
Cake, 106
Coconut Sour Cream

Pound Cake, 117
Easy Coconut
Cake, 105
Franklin Nut
Cake, 107
Fruitcakes, 109
Hawaiian Wedding
Cake, 110
"Hi, Buddy" Butter
Fruitcake, 108
Honey Bun Cake, 110
Honey Spice Chiffon
Cake, 111
Hummingbird
Cake, 112
Key Lime Cake, 113
Light Pound Cake, 118
Melt-in-Your-Mouth
Lemon Loaf
Cakes, 114
Orange Poppy Seed
Cake, 115
Pumpkin Roll, 119
Swedish Butter
Cake, 121
Texas Sheet Cake, 120

Candy
Chocolate
Crunchies, 153
Never-Fail Fudge, 152
Peanut Butter
Balls, 153

Cheese
Asparagus Swiss
Soufflé, 83
Black-Eyed Peas con
Queso, 12
Cheddar Cheese and
Asparagus Soup, 22
Hot Cheese and Crab
Dip, 11
Macaroni with Four
Cheeses, 96

Mozzarella Cheese
Puffs, 9
Pineapple Cheese
Ball, 16
Pizza Rounds, 9
Strawberry Cheese
Ring, 16
Ziti with Vegetables and
Feta Cheese, 97

Chicken
Apricot Chicken, 64
Baked Chicken
Breasts, 64
Cheesy Chicken, 65
Chicken Cacciatore, 66
Chicken Cacciatore
with Egg
Noodles, 65
Chicken Elegant, 69
Chicken Potpie, 67
Chicken Spectacular, 68
Chicken Tetrazzini, 69
Company
Chicken, 70
Microwave Juicy
Chicken, 63
Oven-Roasted
Chicken, 62
Poppy Seed Chicken
Casserole, 63

Chocolate
Chocolate
Crunchies, 153
Chocolate Fudge
Sauce, 135
Chocolate Pecan
Pie, 144
Chocolate Pecan
Turtle Bars, 130
Coffee Charlotte
Russe, 136
Dutch Brick
Dessert, 137

German Chocolate
Pie, 143
Never-Fail Fudge, 152
Next Best Thing
to Robert
Redford, 139
Peanut Butter
Balls, 153
Sheet Cake
Frosting, 120
Special Fudge
Brownies, 124
Texas Sheet Cake, 120
Toffee Bars, 129
Triple-A Bars, 129

Coconut
Coconut Sour Cream
Pound Cake, 117
Easy Coconut
Cake, 105
Hawaiian Wedding
Cake, 110
Impossible Coconut
Pie, 145
Pineapple Coconut
Pie, 150

Cookies
Almond Ginger
Wafers, 122
Apricot Biscotti, 123
Chiffon Nut Bars, 124
Chinese Chews, 125
Chocolate Pecan Turtle
Bars, 130
Christmas Holly
Cookies, 125
Date Bars, 126
Gingersnaps, 127
Mexican Wedding
Cookies, 128
Pecan Balls, 128
Special Fudge
Brownies, 124

Toffee Bars, 129
Triple-A Bars, 129

Corn
Broccoli and Corn
Casserole, 87
Corny Corn Bread, 40
Green Bean and Corn
Casserole, 86
Turkey and Corn
Chowder, 26

Crab Meat
Baked Crab and
Shrimp, 76
Crab and Scallop
Bake, 78
Crab Meat
Soufflé, 77
Crab-Stuffed
Flounder, 72
Deviled Crab, 75
Deviled Crab
Supreme, 74
Hot Cheese and Crab
Dip, 11
Imperial Crab
Casserole, 76

Cranberry
Apple and Cranberry
Casserole, 100
Apple and Cranberry
Relish, 101

Dates
Chinese Chews, 125
Date Bars, 126
Meringue Pie, 145

Desserts
Amaretto
Cheesecake, 132
Apple Dumplings, 133
Boiled Custard, 135

Chocolate Fudge
Sauce, 135
Coffee Charlotte
Russe, 136
Dutch Brick
Dessert, 137
From-Scratch Banana
Pudding, 134
Lemon-Pecan
Dessert, 138
Next Best Thing
to Robert
Redford, 139

Dips
Black-Eyed Peas con
Queso, 12
Guacamole Dip, 12
Hot Artichoke
Dip, 11
Hot Cheese and
Crab Dip, 11
Layered Taco Dip, 14
Rosedale Dip, 15
South-of-the-Border
Dip, 13
Spinach Dip, 15

Fish. *See also* Seafood
Christmas Flounder, 73
Crab-Stuffed
Flounder, 72
Fish with Peas and
Potatoes in Paprika
Sauce, 71
Salmon Bake, 72
Seashell Mold, 32

Frostings
Brown Sugar
Frosting, 111
Cream Cheese and
Pecan Frosting, 112
Cream Cheese
Frosting, 116

Sheet Cake
Frosting, 120

Fruit. *See also* individual
kinds
Banana Nut Bread, 41
Bourbon Peach
Pie, 147
Cherry Cheese Pie, 142
Franklin Nut Cake, 107
From-Scratch Banana
Pudding, 134
Fruitcakes, 109
Grape Salad, 28
"Hi, Buddy" Butter
Fruitcake, 108

Ham
Ham Rolls, 8
Rosy Ham Loaf, 57

**Herbs, Spices and
Edible Flowers**
Allium, 94
Anise Hyssop, 143
Basil, 102
Bee Balm, 61
Borage, 36
Bouquet Garni, 55
Burnet, 18
Buying Herbs and
Spices, 127
Calendula, 39
Capers, 10
Caraway Seeds, 46
Cardamom, 93
Carolina Allspice, 123
Chervil, 17
Cilantro, 13
Cinnamon, 104
Clove Pinks, 149
Cloves, 42
Coriander, 45
Daisy, 137
Dandelion, 82

Daylily, 91
Decorative Herbs, 151
Dill, 74
Dry Mustard, 35
Fennel, 25
Garlic, 80
Ginger, 122
Gingerroot, 101
Harvesting Herbs, 14
Herb ABCs, 126
Herb Seasoning, 138
Herbal Tea, 68
Herbal Vinegars, 33
Hollyhocks, 70
Honeysuckle, 114
Johnny-Jump-Ups, 140
Lavender, 49
Lemon, 19
Lemon Balm, 92
Lilac, 97
Marigold, 54
Marjoram, 77
Mint, 121
Nasturtium, 85
Nutmeg, 141
Orange, 27
Oregano, 37
Pansy, 133
Parsley, 78
Pineapple Sage, 107
Pizza Garden, 67
Queen Anne's
Lace, 117
Rosemary, 89
Rose, 90
Sage, 62
Scented
Geraniums, 146
Squash Blossoms, 86
Storing Herbs, 100
Substitution, 134
Sweet Onions, 38
Sweet Woodruff, 106
Tarragon, 75
Thyme, 60

Tulip, 152
Vanilla, 144
Verbena, 84
Violet, 41
Wax Myrtle, 139
Wild Strawberry, 118

Lemon
Lemon-Pecan
Dessert, 138
Melt-in-Your-Mouth
Lemon Loaf
Cakes, 114

Nuts
Almond Ginger
Wafers, 122
Banana Nut Bread, 41
Black Walnut Pound
Cake, 116
Chiffon Nut
Bars, 124
Chinese Chews, 125
Chocolate Pecan
Pie, 144
Chocolate Pecan Turtle
Bars, 130
Company Pecan
Pie, 148
Cream Cheese and
Pecan Frosting, 112
Date Bars, 126
Franklin Nut
Cake, 107
Lemon Nut Bread, 44
Lemon-Pecan
Dessert, 138
Meringue Pie, 145
Mexican Wedding
Cookies, 128
Nut Bread, 43
Pecan Balls, 128
Pecan Pie, 148
Toffee Bars, 129
Triple-A Bars, 129

Orange
Apricot and Orange
Salad, 27
Easy Orange and
Pineapple Salad, 28
Orange Poppy Seed
Cake, 115

Pasta
Baked Spaghetti, 53
Broccoli with
Noodles, 88
Chicken Cacciatore
with Egg
Noodles, 65
Chicken Tetrazzini, 69
Fettuccini Alfredo, 95
Macaroni with Four
Cheeses, 96
Meat and Cheese
Tortellini Salad, 31
Ziti with Vegetables and
Feta Cheese, 97

Peas
Black-Eyed Peas con
Queso, 12
Fish with Peas and
Potatoes in Paprika
Sauce, 71

Pies
Apple Pie with Crumb
Crust, 141
Bourbon Peach
Pie, 147
Buttermilk Pie, 142
Cherry Cheese
Pie, 142
Chocolate Pecan
Pie, 144
Company Pecan
Pie, 148
German Chocolate
Pie, 143

Impossible Coconut
  Pie, 145
Meringue Pie, 145
Million-Dollar Pie, 146
Old-Fashioned Apple
  Pie, 140
Pecan Pie, 148
Pineapple Chiffon
  Pie, 149
Pineapple Coconut
  Pie, 150
Pumpkin and Bourbon
  Pie for
  Diabetics, 150
Sweet Potato Pie, 151

Pineapple
  Baked Pineapple, 99
  Congealed Pineapple
    Salad, 29
  Easy Orange and
    Pineapple Salad, 28
  Hawaiian Wedding
    Cake, 110
  Hummingbird
    Cake, 112
  Million-Dollar
    Pies, 146
  Pineapple Cheese
    Ball, 16
  Pineapple Chiffon
    Pie, 149
  Pineapple Coconut
    Pie, 150
  Pineapple Salad, 29
  Pineapple Soufflé, 99

Pork
  Baked Pork Chops, 57

Dick Jones' Barbecued
  Pork, 58
Highlands Pork
  Chops, 60
Pizza Rounds, 9
Pork Chops with
  Honey-Mustard
  Sauce, 61
Rosy Ham Loaf, 57

Potatoes
  Different Potato and
    Bean Casserole, 90
  Fish with Peas and
    Potatoes in Paprika
    Sauce, 71
  Hearty Potato Soup, 25
  Potato Casserole, 91

Rice
  Carolina Red Rice, 98
  Mediterranean Rice
    Pilaf, 98

Salads
  Apricot and Orange
    Salad, 27
  Asian Coleslaw, 36
  Bibb Lettuce with
    Soy-Sesame
    Vinaigrette, 34
  Congealed Pineapple
    Salad, 29
  Corn Bread Salad, 34
  Dig-Deep Party
    Salad, 30
  Easy Orange and
    Pineapple Salad, 28
  Easy Tomato Aspic, 32

Grape Salad, 28
Greek Salad, 37
Layered Salad, 38
Marinated Bean
  Salad, 33
Meat and Cheese
  Tortellini Salad, 31
Old South Cabbage
  Slaw, 35
Pineapple Salad, 29
Seashell Mold, 32

Seafood. See also Crab
  Meat; Fish; Shrimp
  Clam Chowder, 24
  Crab and Scallop
    Bake, 78
  Lobster-Stuffed Beef
    Tenderloin, 49
  Scalloped Oysters, 79

Shrimp
  Baked Crab and
    Shrimp, 76
  Garlic Shrimp with
    White Wine, 80
  Pickled Shrimp, 10
  Shrimp Mold, 17
  Shrimp Newburg, 79
  Shrimp Spread, 18

Soups
  Beef and Vegetable
    Soup, 23
  Cheddar Cheese and
    Asparagus Soup, 22
  Clam Chowder, 24
  Hearty Potato Soup, 25
  Squash Soup, 24

Turkey and Corn
  Chowder, 26

Spinach
  Spinach Casserole, 92
  Spinach Dip, 15

Squash
  Squash Casserole, 93
  Squash Soup, 24

Sweet Potatoes
  Norwegian Bread, 45
  Sweet Potato
    Casserole, 94
  Sweet Potato
    Pie, 151

Turkey
  Turkey and Corn
    Chowder, 26

Vegetables. See also
    individual kinds;
    Soups
  Baked Stuffed
    Eggplant, 89
  Black-Eyed Peas con
    Queso, 12
  Dig-Deep Party
    Salad, 30
  Easy Tomato Aspic, 32
  Greek Salad, 37
  Layered Salad, 38
  Vegetable Casserole, 95
  Vegetable Spread, 19
  Ziti with Vegetables and
    Feta Cheese, 97

A Pinch of Thyme

New Hanover Regional Medical Center Gift Shop
P.O. Box 9000 ❧ 2131 South 17th Street ❧ Wilmington, NC 28402–9000

Please send _____ copies of *A Pinch of Thyme* .... $ 16.95 each $ _____

Postage and Handling . . . . $ 3.50 each $ _____

Sales Tax (North Carolina Residents Only) . . . . $ .90 each $ _____

Total $ _____

Method of Payment

[   ] VISA   [   ] MasterCard

Name _____

Account Number _____

Address _____

Expiration Date _____

City _____ State _____ Zip _____

Signature _____

Daytime Phone _____

Make checks payable to New Hanover Regional Medical Center Auxiliary

A Pinch of Thyme

New Hanover Regional Medical Center Gift Shop
P.O. Box 9000 ❧ 2131 South 17th Street ❧ Wilmington, NC 28402–9000

Please send _____ copies of *A Pinch of Thyme* .... $ 16.95 each $ _____

Postage and Handling . . . . $ 3.50 each $ _____

Sales Tax (North Carolina Residents Only) . . . . $ .90 each $ _____

Total $ _____

Method of Payment

[   ] VISA   [   ] MasterCard

Name _____

Account Number _____

Address _____

Expiration Date _____

City _____ State _____ Zip _____

Signature _____

Daytime Phone _____

Make checks payable to New Hanover Regional Medical Center Auxiliary